Praise for *Devoted*

"Dick and Rick prove that the seemingly impossible is possible with every step they take on their awe-inspiring journey. Their unconditional bond of care and support for each other has led to accomplishments beyond the imaginable. They stand alone as a symbol of encouragement to not only the physically challenged, but to us all."

—**Uta Pippig, three-time winner of both the Boston and Berlin Marathons, and President of Take The Magic Step®**

"It is incredible what can happen when a parent and child unite in an effort to find a shared passion as Dick and Rick Hoyt have. Through very hard work they have become a powerful part of this sport of running. Their story is truly uplifting!"

—**Bill Rodgers, four-time winner of the Boston Marathon and the New York City Marathon**

"When I saw Dick Hoyt racing for the first time on TV, I thought, 'This man is an animal,' and I asked myself, 'How can this be possible?' There's a famous saying commonly used back home in Slovakia: 'Love can move the mountains.' And that's exactly what Dick did for his son Rick. I've never met anybody who worked harder than Dick and Rick Hoyt. This book is an unbelievable story; it goes way beyond just racing, it defines what the true meaning of passion really is."

—**Zdeno Chara, Boston Bruins**

Devoted

The Story of a Father's Love for His Son

Dick Hoyt
with Don Yaeger

"Enjoy The Book"

Rick + Dick Hoyt

Da Capo Press
A Member of the Perseus Books Group

Copyright © 2010 by Dick Hoyt

All rights reserved. No part of this publication may be reproduced, stored in a retrieval system, or transmitted, in any form or by any means, electronic, mechanical, photocopying, recording, or otherwise, without the prior written permission of the publisher. Printed in the United States of America. For information, address Da Capo Press, 44 Farnsworth Street, 3rd Floor, Boston, MA 02210.

Design and production by Eclipse Publishing Services
Set in 10-point Janson

Cataloging-in-Publication data for this book is available from the Library of Congress.

ISBN: 978-0-306-81832-5 (hardcover)
ISBN: 978-0-306-82074-8 (paperback)

First Da Capo Press edition 2010
First Da Capo Press paperback edition 2012

Published by Da Capo Press
A Member of the Perseus Books Group
www.dacapopress.com

Da Capo Press books are available at special discounts for bulk purchases in the U.S. by corporations, institutions, and other organizations. For more information, please contact the Special Markets Department at the Perseus Books Group, 2300 Chestnut Street, Suite 200, Philadelphia, PA 19103, or call (800) 810-4145, ext. 5000, or e-mail special.markets@perseusbooks.com.

10 9 8 7 6 5 4 3

I would like to dedicate this book to my mother and father,

who have always supported us. They are the ones who provided me with a strong heart and body that enabled us to compete at a level beyond my own expectations and explanation.

I also dedicate the book to Judy, Rick's mother,

who fought bravely and tirelessly to assure Rick an education, one that truly enabled him to be included in all daily activities.

And to my sons Rob and Russ,

who selflessly accepted the fact that Rick's requirements created hardships on them at times, and frequently denied them the attention they deserved. I am very proud of who they are and what they have become.

Also to Kathy Boyer,

my girlfriend and office manager, who has spent many hours researching material for this book as well as proofing, editing, and rewriting to make sure the story being told is accurate.

First and foremost, however, I dedicate this book to my son Rick.

If it were not for his inner strength and determination, there would be no book. He is the one who inspires and motivates me. He is the heart and soul of Team Hoyt.

— Dick Hoyt

To Jeanette:

Thanks for inspiring me to be a great father . . . and for giving me that opportunity! I hope I am as successful with our two as Dick has been with Rick.

— Don Yaeger

Contents

Contents

Acknowledgments

Devoted has taken more than two years to complete, including countless hours of interviews, compiling information, writing, and editing. We hope the book will inspire and motivate people around the world. I especially wish to thank the following for all their help and support:

New York Times bestselling author Don Yaeger, and Jessica Pitchford, a Ph. D. candidate in Florida State University's Creative Writing Program, who spent many, many hours making this such a wonderful book. Also, Jenny Fernandez and Lauren Held for keeping the project organized and on schedule.

This book would not have happened without the team at Da Capo Press, most notably editor Kevin Hanover. They believed in this story from the start and have made it possible to share our story with readers. Thanks again to all of you for your help!

All the doctors, nurses, and therapists from Children's Hospital Boston, and the engineers from Tufts University who built Rick his first communication machine—the Tufts Interactive Communicator (TIC).

All of our family, friends, and neighbors who have supported us through the years.

Mike Giallongo and XRE—the company in Littleton, Massachusetts, that was our first sponsor. XRE built our first bike so we could start competing in triathlons. Mike was also the first president of the Hoyt Fund.

Eddie Burke—a great supporter of Team Hoyt and the Race Director of our Annual Team Hoyt Road Race.

Dave McGillivray—the first person to suggest we compete in triathlons. Dave also convinced the Ironman organization to allow us to compete in the Ironman Triathlon World Championship.

All of Rick's Personal Care Assistants (PCAs) whom he has worked with over the years. If it was not for them, Rick would never have been able to live an independent life.

Pete Wisnewski—the first person to approach and encourage me and Rick at our first race. He became a lifelong friend.

John Costello—the Director of the Augmentative Communication Program at Children's Hospital Boston. John has worked with Rick since 1986, and because of his support Rick has the excellent communication system that has enabled him to express his thoughts to the world.

Devoted

Internet Sensation

I had heard the phrase *Internet sensation* before but never truly understood the meaning. Now I do. No one would ever mistake me for a computer whiz; I barely know how to check e-mail. My grandkids talk about online networking and chatting and blogs, tech-speak way beyond my comprehension. These days, though, you can't turn on the television or listen to the news without a mention of how the Internet is changing our lives. And lately, the lives being changed are those of average people whose stories somehow inspire hope. I never imagined that our story would be one of them.

My eldest son, Rick, had been wheelchair-bound for over a decade the first time he asked me to put on a pair of running shoes and push him in a race. The year was 1977. I was thirty-seven years old and hadn't seriously exercised since high school. I jogged a couple times a week and played on a pickup hockey team when I had time, but other than that, I just worked for the National Guard and tried to spend as much time with my family as possible. My first race with Rick was exhilarating, but extremely difficult. We didn't come in last, but by the time we finally crossed the finish line, I was huffing and puffing. Muscles hurt that I didn't even know I had. When we got home, all I wanted to do was relax, but Rick went straight to his communication device, called a "Tufts Interactive Communication Device," or "TIC," and told me how much he had loved the experience. I knew right then we had discovered something special for the two of us to share. Dick and Rick became a father-son team—Team Hoyt. From that day forward, each race we've run together has only strengthened our bond.

By the time the average household was equipped with Internet access, we'd been racing for twenty-five years—so long that many people had already heard our story. Though our fans were limited mostly to the running world, we'd done interviews both locally and nationally. Rosie O'Donnell interviewed us for her talk show, and *Parade* magazine had done a little piece about us. A *Sports Illustrated* article on Father's Day, 2005, really took the cake, though. That article had more impact than any other article ever written about us. Rick Reilly's words really capture the love that my son and I have for each other and the hard work it took for us to get where we are today. But still, I always considered Team Hoyt a novelty item. Only certain groups—generally those who could relate to Rick's disability and what we went through with him as a family—could truly appreciate us. That was, until September 2006, when an online video changed our lives.

I was preparing myself for the Hawaii Ironman Triathlon and had just finished up a long day of training. I came home expecting to relax and rest up for another day of running, swimming, and biking, but as soon as I walked in the door, Kathy Boyer, my girlfriend and the manager of my business, called to me from the office we have set up in my home (I do corporate motivational speaking). She said I needed to see something.

I found her, sitting at the computer and staring at a screen full of e-mails. I knew she'd been a little stressed, managing the office work and preparing for our Hawaii trip only weeks away, but I couldn't imagine what could have her this frazzled. A glitch in our schedule? Trouble packing Rick's equipment? I was way off! Turned out she was receiving so many e-mails that her inbox was completely full, and she didn't know how to begin to respond. Kathy is great at her job—one of the most organized people I've ever met. I know how important it is to her that she answer all the messages that come in, as quickly as possible. "Every time I turn around," she said, "there are fifteen or twenty more. They just keep coming." It had gotten so bad, she told me, that she'd had to shut off her speakers so her computer would quit announcing the arrival of new mail. Even I knew this was unusual.

The reason for all the e-mails, I soon found out, was a video of Rick and me racing that had been circulating the Internet. Kathy told me that people had been e-mailing and faxing her letters about how they'd seen Team Hoyt on YouTube and just had to write to us. It started with one fan, and then strangers began contacting us, all saying the same thing—how inspired they had been by the

YouTube video and our story. My first thought was, "YouTube? What in the heck is YouTube?"

Then I pulled up a chair and Kathy went to youtube.com, typed in "Team Hoyt," and quickly found the clip everyone was talking about. There was the "Redeemer" DVD that the World Triathlon Corporation (owner of Ironman) had made of us back in 2004. It's a five-minute video that contains clips of Rick and me swimming, biking, and running in the 1999 Ironman Triathlon in Hawaii, set to the song "My Redeemer Lives." I remember the first time I saw it, thinking, "So that's what we must look like to other people." There's me—with the sandy graying hair and wrinkled skin expected of a man my age—and there's Rick, who at forty-something appears strikingly young and so happy from his spot in his specialized running chair or inflatable boat. I remember being proud to see us in action.

I couldn't understand what a video of Rick and me was doing on the Internet for all to see and comment on. We were amazed that the clip had found its way to YouTube. By then, several thousand people had viewed it. Over the next couple of weeks, Kathy would check in occasionally, and in no time, it was up to one million hits. Other popular clips on the site didn't come close to this. The e-mails kept pouring in, so many that Kathy had to wait until after our trip to Hawaii to respond. I hardly knew what to make of it. I'm not a guy easily rattled; you have to remember that we were preparing for the World Championship Ironman Triathlon in Hawaii, so I was in competition mode. I went right back to training and didn't give it a whole lot of thought. I let Kathy handle the business matters, so Rick and I can focus on racing.

After a few months, we realized that people were downloading the clip and even selling it. Others were using it at events without our permission. To this day, we have no idea how the video arrived at YouTube or who was responsible for posting it. Since WTC Ironman owns the copyright, they pulled it from YouTube several times, but it kept popping up again. I think they just gave up. I've heard that there are now nine or ten YouTube videos of Team Hoyt, set to a variety of songs and in multiple languages. YouTube visitors can find clips from the *Today Show* and *HBO Real Sports*, too.

I rarely sat at the computer and didn't know how to navigate to Web sites, so it took a while for all this to sink in. I wasn't angry that we seemed to be all over the Web. It was more humbling than anything. The e-mails we were receiving and continue to receive are from people from every walk of life—those in the military who've seen war action, police officers who've witnessed terrible things in the line of duty, children who haven't spoken to their parents in years, parents who spend too much time in the office instead of at home—and they're all taking the time to write us and say that our story has inspired them to make some changes and be better people. It's mind boggling to realize we could have that kind of impact.

When we came home from the 2006 Hawaii Ironman, Kathy began the slow process of responding to people's mails. She put aside special messages if they were asking about a running chair like Team Hoyt's or a communication computer like Rick's. Kathy forwards e-mail about communication devices to John Costello from Children's Hospital Boston. He answers them and finds someone in their area to get them an assessment appointment for their children to see if they can use a device like Rick's. We've also collected a lot of information on running chairs and bikes that people have sent us over the years, so we try to return the favor and share that with others when they ask us about equipment similar to ours.

We hear incredible stories from so many of the people—some claiming to be overweight couch potatoes now trying to get active and run races, people who say they have given up abusing their bodies with drugs and alcohol, persons with disabilities who no longer want to suffer limitations. And they all thank us for being an inspiration. It's hard to process the magnitude of the whole thing—that technology could let so many people in so many different parts of the world see a video and respond to it. We hear from strangers across the globe—from Toronto to Tokyo. Fans tell us they have lined the Boston Marathon route for the last twenty-seven years to cheer on Rick and me. We always thought that it would be awesome if we could help one person, but now it seems we're helping countless numbers of people. It's unbelievable. And it's all largely due to the Internet.

Eventually, somebody took that original "Redeemer" DVD and changed it a bit, featuring Rick's computer screen with the word *Can* across it (a play on our motto, "Yes You Can"), and set the images to the song "I Can Only Imagine." Kathy got so many requests for a DVD with that music that she contacted WTC Ironman. They were able to get the rights to the song from the group Mercy Me. In 2007, WTC Ironman then produced the "CAN" DVD set to "I Can Only Imagine." It is basically the same footage that's shown on the "Redeemer" DVD, but the focus is our can-do attitude, and there's different music. Both DVDs are very popular, and people worldwide show them during church services, business meetings, and sports practices to motivate their viewers. Of course, thanks to YouTube, individuals sitting at home in front of their computer screens have seen the videos and have been moved to comment and then forward them on to their friends and family.

It's still hard for me to make sense of. I think people latch onto the Team Hoyt story because these days there are so many bad stories out there. You hear about killings, war, drugs, and abuse so much that it is nice to finally see a story that really is about love and dedication. Rick is my inspiration, so I can empathize with that feeling to want to hear some good news for a change. For me, he puts things in perspective. I don't have bad days because I know that life can go on, and you simply have to make the best out of the situation you are handed. I love my son, and there isn't anything I would not do for him—and he for me. We race not because we have to, but because we want to. If that inspires others, I'm even happier for it.

Rick and I try hard to keep a positive outlook on life. We firmly believe that the things we have accomplished over the years are because we wanted them badly enough and set our minds to it, no matter if it was finding a way to communicate, getting an education, finishing an Ironman triathlon, or biking and running across the United States. We didn't bargain that we might be able to help others in the process. All these years, I was just running, enjoying the time with my son—the love, the bond, every good feeling that comes with the effort we put forth when we're competing.

The world of technology changed our lives. When I realized our story was touching people, it made me feel even better about all that Rick and I have accomplished. It's brought our story to millions. Although it wasn't what we set out to do, we're so pleased that it happened.

For that reason, we wanted to devote a few of the pages in this book to several people whose lives we've touched. Their stories, featured at the end of chapters 14 through 17, demonstrate just how far a little inspiration can travel. In turn, their stories are inspiring others—including us—every day.

The four stories featured in this book are just a few of the many that have come to us in letters or emails over the last 25 years.

Chapter 1

My Story

I was born on June 1, 1940, in Winchester, Massachusetts, the sixth of ten children. There were five boys and five girls in the Hoyt clan, and we all entered the world in the same Winchester hospital where my children and even some of my children's children would eventually be born. My nine brothers and sisters and I grew up in tight quarters in a small house in nearby North Reading, fifteen miles north of downtown Boston. All of us were blond and blue-eyed. We were known in our community as a very healthy, active family, despite having to eat in shifts and live in a tiny home with only one bathroom. Still, it was a normal upbringing with two loving, hardworking parents, and probably nothing unusual for the era. My parents, Anne and Alfred Hoyt, were salt-of-the-earth people who were married for a lifetime. They weren't particularly strict with us, though with all those mouths to feed, we were expected to do our part to pitch in, whether that meant helping my mother around the house or doing manual labor with my father. My duties tended to be manual tasks, a work pattern that would follow me into adulthood.

I've always liked a challenge and enjoyed working with my hands. It was rewarding to create something the hard way. We had to heat our house with a wood- or coal-burning stove, so when I was old enough, I was responsible for chopping down trees to stoke the fire. I landed my first real job when I was nine years old at a local farm called Eisenhower's Farm, about a two-mile walk from our home. I got ten cents a day and a half pint of milk for bringing the cows in from the pasture, milking the cows, plus shoveling the manure and pitching hay.

When I was twelve years old, I got fifty cents an hour working for a local produce farmer who had fields in both my hometown of North Reading and in nearby Topsfield, Massachusetts. I weeded crops, picked produce and did whatever else he needed done in his fields. When the farmer needed help at his fields in Topsfield, he loaded three or four of us kids in his pickup truck and drove us there in the morning, and then drove us back to North Reading at the end of the day when our chores were finished. From then on, I always had some kind of job to keep me busy while earning a little pocket money. By the time I got to high school, I'd done farm labor, worked at a local filling station, and held cleanup and handyman jobs. Some days, I'd put in twelve hours and earn as much as $18. I thought I was rich! I imagined I was doing so well getting $3 an hour working summers as a brick mason that I dropped out of school my junior year to work full time. That lasted about a year before I realized how important it was to finish school, and I returned to North Reading High—much to the delight of my parents. Even though I relished the hard jobs, there was lighter work, too, like when I was soda jerk at Price's Drug. I had fun, working behind the counter. I wouldn't let the kids who'd come in refer to me as "the Jerk" though. I had learned that you earn respect when you work for it.

The Hoyts were a physically active bunch, but it wasn't until I was eleven or twelve that I started playing sports. Before then, being right in the middle of the Hoyt lineup, I had all my brothers and sisters to keep me entertained. We were a close-knit family and did a lot of things together, both play and work. With so many children running around and my dad supporting his large family as a car salesman, we were pretty poor. It never really felt as if we were doing without, but looking back now, our make-do financial situation was evident. For instance, if we wanted to play hockey, we had to share one pair of skates. We'd have to cut a branch off a tree to use as a hockey stick, and a piece of wood was our stand-in for a puck. It wasn't any big deal to us; we loved the game, however we got to play it.

Sports were a large part of our lives, and our parents always encouraged us in athletics. They were hardworking, athletic people themselves. You had to be to keep up with ten kids, I guess! They gave us our freedom, but also expected us to obey the house rules. Whenever we got out of line, Mom wouldn't wait for Dad to come home and deal with us. She just picked up the broomstick and chased us around the house. Lucky for me, I could outrun her. The amazing thing was that my parents found time for each of us. They expected us to do big things. Anne Hoyt was an extremely dedicated mother who ran an efficient household. She had a lot of pride and love for every one of us and told us so often. To this day I try to maintain the strong bonds she instilled in us. For example, once a year I get the entire family together for an annual cookout at my house—all the siblings, their kids, and grandkids.

My dad always expected that my accomplishments would have something to do with athletics. He always steered me toward sports, and when he had time off, we'd listen to a ballgame on the radio or play catch in the backyard. Maybe it was because he secretly considered himself an athlete or perhaps it was simply something rooted in his own childhood and the nature of games then. Dad loved sports more than anyone I knew. His greatest hope for his children was that one of us might become a professional athlete. When I was a young man, barely an adult and holding on to dreams of a sports career, I remember Dad telling me, "You'll know you've made it as an athlete when you're on *Wide World of Sports*." I finally made an appearance on the program in 1989, but sadly my father had passed away three years earlier. Alfred Hoyt was a great role model, the kind of father many children never have. He had long been my biggest fan, and I took his death hard. Throughout his life, no matter what I was doing or what obstacles I faced, his confidence in me never waned. I respected him for being such a supportive father. I have tried my best to pass his outlook on to my own sons.

Thanks in part to my parents' encouragement and natural athletic ability, organized sports were practically all I thought about when I was old enough to participate. Until sixth grade, I had made straight As. Then I got into athletics. I also found out about girls. I got sidetracked a little and even had my girlfriend do my homework for me in seventh grade, but then I buckled down in eighth grade and realized that I needed to do my own work. I was smart, but clearly my interests lay in sports. By the end of eighth grade, I'd played football, basketball, and baseball. The school awarded me a plaque for being the best all-around student. I'd held offices in the Student Council, the Leader's Club, and the Boy's Club, served as business manager of the yearbook, and was even a Junior Rotarian. Though I managed to earn good grades and had a full social calendar, I got the biggest thrill out of sports, and that's where I really excelled.

I was a little guy. At age fourteen, I probably weighed ninety pounds soaking wet. However, my slight stature was my secret weapon. I may have been small, but I was powerful. Freshman year I was playing middle linebacker and fullback on the varsity football team. I could always pick up a yard or two. Sometimes the coach would put me at tight end. No one would cover me because I was so little; they didn't think I posed a threat. So my teammates would throw me the ball, and I'd score touchdowns. Everyone—at least those supporting the home team—got a kick out of the surprise attack.

In North Reading, we had three school sports—football, basketball, and baseball. With fifty kids in my graduating class, there were only eleven players on the football team, so we all saw a lot of playing time and had to cover a variety of positions. My teammates and I often got hurt, but we loved the game. I was captain of the football and baseball teams. I was a fairly strong football player, but my power sport was baseball. I played catcher, had a strong arm, and could hit, too.

In my senior year, my best friend John Staff, North Reading High's shortstop, and I were invited to try out for the New York

Yankees. It was incredible—two kids from a town no one had ever heard of, playing in the big leagues. We went to a camp with thirty-five hundred other people from a lot of big schools. We were there for three days, playing with some of best talent from across the nation. I threw a couple of times the second day, was timed running to first base, and got to bat twice. That was pretty much it for the whole weekend, but my buddy and I were thrilled to go. Just being away from home was an experience. Though we didn't make the team, it was an honor to try out. Back in North Reading, I fixed my attention on sports. Between working part-time after school as a mason tender, school, and extracurricular activities, I didn't get a whole lot of sleep. But it was sure fun.

I was busy, but not so busy that I didn't have time to take an interest in girls, and one in particular. Judy Lieghton was the captain of the cheerleading squad. I'd known her since seventh grade, but we didn't become an item until high school. Judy was a beautiful girl, ambitious, confident, and outgoing. I was quiet and tended to follow the crowd. She had a lot of friends. So did I. In our small town, we ran in similar circles. I found that when Judy wanted something, she went after it until she got it. It took a while for me to catch on. She'd always try to dance with me when I'd show up at the popular North Reading Friday night dances, but I had my friends cut in when we were dancing together. I liked her, but I was very shy and didn't know what to say to her. Eventually, however, I loosened up and was able to talk to Judy, and we became high school sweethearts. We were sixteen, and it was the first time either of us had been in love. When we graduated in 1959, we were voted Class Couple. In the yearbook, next to our photos, it says, "Judy and Richie are like coffee and tea. One without the other you will rarely see." It was a silly little rhyme but true. Once we started dating, we remained inseparable.

After I graduated from high school, it became clear that I hadn't prepared myself for college. I was nervous about the next step and uncertain if I even wanted to go to college, so I fell back on my old failsafe—manual labor. I returned to the masonry business as a bricklayer, building chimneys and fireplaces. Though I enjoyed the work, I didn't want to make it my career. More and more, I'd been thinking about joining the military. My brother-in-law, Paul Sweeney, suggested that instead of going on active duty, I look into the National Guard. I figured if I liked it, I could keep doing it, and if I didn't, I could go on to active duty or come home and find work.

I went off to six months of basic training at Fort Dix, New Jersey, and loved it. A lot of the other guys in training hated the daily regimen of military training, but I always seemed to do well with things that were tough. I got the highest physical-training award and graduated at the top of my outfit. At the end of training, we took tests to determine our next orders. Because I tested highest in electronics, they sent me to Fort Bliss, Texas, to a guided-missile school for advanced training. Only a few of us from basic training had qualified. Everyone started off by doing KP and guard duty for a week. That part was awful. It wasn't what I wanted to do, but I soon advanced in the ranks and received an appointment to platoon sergeant.

Four months later, the National Guard shipped me to Milton Nike Site in Milton, Massachusetts, just one of the Nike missile sites in the United States that had an air-defense system to combat the new jet aircraft with Ajax and Hercules missiles. I worked full-time as a missile controller in Milton on the Nike

Ajax system before they transferred me to Reading. While there, I was promoted and sent for additional training in El Paso, Texas, on the new Nike Hercules system. Finally, the army sent me back to Lincoln, Massachusetts.

Throughout our training, my fellow comrades and I were full-time guardsmen and were treated as if we were on active duty. We reported to the active army chain of command. We wore the army uniform and performed the same job as active duty people. The only difference was that we didn't go overseas. Instead, I worked at various missile sites in Massachusetts. When I found out about openings at other missile sites that would advance my career, I would apply for them. I progressed pretty rapidly in the enlisted ranks. One of my commanders thought I was good officer material, so he suggested I go through Officers Candidate School. I got commissioned, and when the missile sites closed I ended up transferring to Otis Air Force Base on Cape Cod, Massachusetts, and then switched to the Air National Guard. So I wound up making a career in the military.

While the military was shipping me around to learn advanced electronics, Judy was back in North Reading in secretarial school. We had stayed in touch while I was away, writing letters and visiting on the holidays. She graduated and went to work for General Electric. When I returned from training as a full-time soldier, we decided it was time to take our relationship to the next level. On February 18, 1961, Judy and I got married. At the time I was stationed in Milton, Massachusetts, about an hour drive from our hometown. I was barely twenty years old, and she was nineteen.

We were young and in love, but we were also practical. We'd both begun new careers, and with the military promising to keep moving me around for more training, we thought it best to save our money and buy a house before adding to the family. That thought didn't last long—a year, to be exact. Judy and I were elated when we found out she was pregnant. We bought a home in North Reading for $11,000, and I got back to working with my hands, making improvements on our new house. Board by board and brick by brick, I remodeled our first home to make it just perfect. I sawed down a wall and built a fireplace and chimney. I put in a big picture window. Some buddies helped me dig a cellar.

Before long, the house was complete and ready for our new family. Everything seemed to fall perfectly into place. The house was done. Judy's pregnancy had gone extremely well. The baby was so active in the womb that we both knew we'd soon have another athlete in the family. We couldn't have been happier or more excited. All we had to do was await the arrival of our baby.

Chapter 2

Rick's Birth

We had always known we wanted children, lots of them. Maybe it was my youth and parenting inexperience talking, but I imagined we would ultimately have a brood that rivaled the one in which I had been raised. Growing up with all those brothers and sisters had been such a positive experience for me that I wanted the same for my own children. I had high hopes for a football team, but I would have settled for a hockey team.

Regardless of how many little ones we ended up with, Judy and I were both over the moon about becoming parents for the first time. We knew this was only the start of our family. It seemed natural. Other people our age were doing the same as us—getting married and beginning a life together. It was a thrilling time in our young lives. Judy and I both had stable jobs that we enjoyed, supportive families, and good friends. By all accounts, we were happy, healthy, and in love. Amid all the excitement, it's possible that we approached parenthood somewhat blinded by our joy. But who could blame us; everything seemed to be coming together perfectly. Little did we know that life could change drastically in a matter of moments. If, as the saying goes, there is no manual for teaching parents how to do their job, there was certainly no manual for what we were about to face.

On January 10, 1962, the Boston Bruins lost to the Toronto Maple Leafs by a score of seven to five, and my first child, Richard Eugene Hoyt Jr. was born, two weeks after Judy's due date. Rick came into this world at Winchester Hospital, the same hospital where my mother had given birth to me twenty-one years before. I was late meeting my firstborn, because I was at work at the army base about an hour away in Milton when Rick arrived. I had taken Judy to the hospital in the wee hours of the morning when she awoke with contractions. Once we had checked in and a nurse wheeled Judy off to a private room, our family doctor said that, given that it was Judy's first labor, there was no telling how long it might take. He suggested that I might as well report to work instead of waiting for what could be the whole day. In those days, fathers weren't allowed in the delivery room. So we trusted that the doctor knew best and that Judy's delivery would take its course and go as smoothly as her uneventful pregnancy. I kissed Judy goodbye and headed for work with the doctor's promise that he would be the first one to call me.

At work on the base, I could hardly concentrate. I was so excited about becoming a father for the first time. I kept thinking about the new adventure Judy and I were embarking on. It wasn't that long ago that we had been kids ourselves, the high school golden couple. She had been the head cheerleader chasing after the captain of the football team. Now we were about to have a baby. I was filled with nervous anticipation.

The call I expected came later that morning. But what I heard was completely unexpected. First, the doctor told me that I had a son. I wanted to shout the news throughout my command post. I envisioned the next eighteen years—my son and I playing catch or tackle football or knocking a puck around on the driveway. But then the doctor explained that there had been a complication during the delivery. Judy was stable and recovering, but our son was showing signs of problems. I could tell by the doctor's tone that the situation was serious. When I pressed him for details, he couldn't seem to give me a straight answer. He suggested that everything could be fine, that Rick could be just like all other babies. At the same time, he didn't want to give me a false sense of hope. My mind was racing with what this might possibly mean. I was in shock and couldn't make sense of it. What problems? How could this have happened? We'd done nothing wrong. Judy had been healthy throughout her pregnancy. More than anything, I was worried about my wife and newborn son. I hung up the phone, feeling confused and frightened and wanting to get to my family as fast as I could. That drive to Winchester was the longest hour of my life.

When I arrived at the hospital, Judy was still sedated because of the medication they had given her, and she couldn't tell me much about what had happened. She knew that our son had been very active while he was being born and that the doctors had some trouble getting him out. They'd had to do a lot of reaching and turning, trying to get him to come out right. She remembered it being frantic in the delivery room toward the end of the birth, with nurses swarming and doctors talking in concerned voices. When they finally did deliver the baby, Judy didn't hear any crying or sounds from the baby. They wouldn't let her hold him, so she had barely gotten a glimpse of him before they whisked him away. "The doctor said he'll be fine," she kept saying. "He's going to be fine."

She was upset that she wasn't able to have the baby with her. All the other new mothers had their babies with them and were able to feed them, talk to them, and get to know them. Judy was crushed that she couldn't do the same. Here we were, two new parents without a clue what was going on and without our child. Neither of us could understand what had gone wrong. While Judy slept and recovered, I remained cautiously optimistic. I paced the hallway, drinking stale coffee and expecting to hear from a nurse or doctor at any moment that our son, our little athlete, was doing just fine. For what felt like an eternity, I received no other news. No one would talk to me, and I couldn't find anyone who seemed to know where our son was or what was wrong with him. Finally, a nurse came and took me to a different area of the hospital, to the neonatal intensive care unit. I had to scrub and put a smock on over my clothes before I was allowed to meet our baby for the first time.

I breathed a sigh of relief when I saw him lying in the incubator. He was a beautiful baby—big and healthy looking and without any hint of the red, splotchy skin most babies have. I don't know what I was expecting, but he appeared healthy to me. In fact, lying on his stomach, he seemed as active as he'd been in the womb, stretching and pumping his arms and legs. It was almost as if he were doing push-ups. I got a kick out of that, thinking happily that he was already preparing for a sports career. I later found out he was having muscle spasms. His muscles seemed very tight. I could tell he was straining, and I wanted to tell him that it was okay to relax, that he didn't have to work so hard. I asked the nurse why he was moving like this and why he had to be in an incubator. She said that they were still running tests to figure out exactly what was wrong with Rick, but what I called push-ups were likely muscle spasms. She told me that the baby had been placed in the incubator because he had been having trouble breathing. In the incubator, they could control the flow of oxygen and monitor him closely while they continued their tests. The explanation worried me, but it sounded like only a precautionary measure, a follow-up for whatever complications had occurred during birth. After seeing our gorgeous boy, I couldn't fathom anything could possibly be wrong. To my eyes, everything looked right.

Back in Judy's hospital room, I reported what I'd seen—that we had a beautiful boy who looked healthy to me. I told her what the nurse had said about his breathing and the muscle spasms, but I assured Judy that the baby looked good and that we shouldn't worry until we received some sort of official diagnosis. Then the doctor who had delivered our baby came in the room and explained the extent of the complications during the birth and what they knew so far about our baby's condition. Finally, we got some answers. The news we heard was conclusive and devastating. There was definitely something wrong with Rick, but they would have to continue the tests to determine what prognosis we might expect. They knew that Rick had been active during birth as he had been in his mother's womb. Before delivery, he had turned over, facing the wrong way with the umbilical cord wrapped around his neck and cutting off oxygen to his brain. He had, in effect, strangled himself. Those few minutes it had taken for the doctor to untangle the cord had done irreparable brain damage.

Judy and I were stunned. Brain damage? What did this mean for his future? The doctor could only tell us that early tests indicated our baby had no physical control over his limbs and in all likelihood never would. He was breathing on his own, but it was labored. The incubator seemed to be helping. In addition, they were having trouble feeding him from a bottle. We had so many unanswered questions. We didn't know what specific disease or disability our baby had or how long it would affect him. Judy and I were far from being trained medical professionals, and it was difficult to process what we'd been told. We were twenty-somethings who had had hopes for a long, happy future with our son. Now we feared that our dreams had been dashed.

This was the early 1960s, before new advances in medical technology. The doctor-patient relationship wasn't as open as it is now. Ordinary people didn't have access to information via the Internet or the Discovery channel. We only knew what our mothers had told us from their experience, and this wasn't a topic that came up often in conversation. Women became pregnant and gave birth to healthy babies all the time, without the benefits of modern technology. The extent of prenatal care was vitamins and physical checkups. Ultrasounds were just being developed for use in obstetrics, and there was no way to see your baby while still in the womb. During labor, women were rarely hooked to fetal monitors, so emergency Caesareans were unheard of. Surgeons certainly didn't schedule C-sections in advance of labor. Without the aid of monitors during the birth, there was no way of knowing whether a baby was in distress. In most cases, you'd simply go into the hospital and come out a few days later with a baby.

Our baby had been fine five minutes before he was born because the cord wasn't then wrapped around his neck. Realizing that we had almost had a healthy baby was probably the hardest blow of all. But these things happen, and that was eventually the attitude my wife and I adopted. We had to. It would have been too painful otherwise. We had been dealt a tough hand, but we knew that we had to find a way to move on.

When the doctor left us alone after delivering the news, Judy and I had a good cry. Then we had a serious conversation. At that point, we hadn't even filled out the birth certificate and given our son his name. Months before, we had decided that if we had a boy, he would be a junior. I'll never forget the look on my wife's face when she asked me if, given the circumstances, I still wanted to name our firstborn son after me. I didn't hesitate. "You bet your life I do," I told her. I was resolved that we were going to come through this triumphant and that our son was going to be a normal child with two loving parents. I knew it wasn't going to be easy, but this was my boy, my namesake. I loved him from the moment I saw him. I was determined to be the best father I could, regardless of whether he had a disability.

We went through a lot of emotions in those early days after Rick's birth. Judy resented the other mothers for being able to take home healthy babies while we were still waiting to learn our son's fate. We had so many unanswered questions. She worried about whether she could handle the care of a disabled child. We talked about finances and whether we could afford to provide the kind of care a disabled child would need. We even got angry with one another, although we both knew deep down that neither of us was to blame for what had happened. It had been unpreventable. Several times, we discussed the possibility that Rick might not survive. I knew that in a corner of Judy's mind, she sensed that Rick's death might be for the best and that she prayed for God to take away our baby's pain and lift the burden of raising him from her shoulders. The situation was extremely trying, and it took a lot out of everyone. It was hard not to be resentful. People deal with life's curveballs differently, and this was the biggest curveball that Judy and I could have ever been thrown. We felt cheated. This was not what we had planned at all.

With nothing to do but wait for test results, I went back to work. Mounting medical bills made that a necessity. Judy remained in the hospital a few more days, recovering from the delivery. I visited as often as I could, but the doctors were hesitant to let us handle the baby too much. I guess they didn't think it was safe until they'd done more tests. It was two more weeks before we would take Rick home. Meanwhile, our families rallied behind us. My mother, having given birth to ten very healthy children in the same hospital, was baffled and upset that the doctors couldn't or wouldn't give us more answers. She made dozens of phone calls to the hospital, trying to find someone to talk to her. It seemed to both our families that anytime we attempted to get answers from the medical personnel, we were ignored or shut out.

The only advice doctors seemed to be able to offer was that we wait and see what happened. We weren't satisfied, but there was simply nothing else to do. For a while, the doctors said that Rick would get better treatment at the hospital than at home, but after all we had been through, there was no way we were going to leave Rick there. Finally, when it became clear we weren't going to get any definite answers soon, the doctors gave in—or gave up. They told us to take Rick home, just as if he were a regular baby. We were overjoyed to finally have our boy with us, although the thought of the unknown and how our son would do when he got home was daunting. In many ways, I think we were in denial. We'd decided that Rick was going to be okay, and that once he was home with us, we'd be a normal, healthy, happy family.

As we drove up to the house with Rick in tow that day in late January, he stayed quiet in Judy's arms. I watched as he squirmed and twisted his body, not making a sound. For a split second, I wondered if we were ready for this. I kept thinking about my own childhood. What a carefree kid I'd been, with all the opportunities I'd had despite growing up in a large family on a tight budget. I realized how lucky we'd all been to be so healthy and active. It had been exactly the kind of life I wanted to provide my children.

Everyone says a child changes your life. We knew that our son Rick was about to change our lives in ways we never could have predicted.

Chapter 3

Diagnosis

Those first few months with Rick at home were painful, especially for Judy. At least I could go to work every day and keep my mind on something else. But she was with Rick all day, every day. Though we still hoped for improvement—and every evening when I came home from work I expected to hear that our son was better, that he was smiling or cooing or starting to roll over—it quickly became clear that something was very wrong with our baby.

For starters, Rick never cried. It wasn't that he was a calm baby. He couldn't cry and couldn't make much noise at all. Then there were the eating issues. We had a lot of trouble getting Rick to eat. He'd spit everything up and couldn't seem to swallow milk successfully. He slept a lot, though it was a fitful sleep with his arms and legs often flailing and his fists constantly clenched. And he wouldn't wake up for feedings. At night, we'd have to set the alarm clock to be sure we got up at his scheduled feeding time. Then we'd have to tickle his feet to wake him enough to feed him.

We took everything day by day. Although we reported our concerns to the family doctor and began taking Rick for frequent checkups at the hospital in Winchester, we still weren't getting any medical answers. Not even our family doctor could tell us what was going to happen. It was frustrating, but there wasn't much else we could do except move forward, keep pushing for answers and hope for improvement.

Judy and I had enough experience with babies of friends and family members to know that Rick wasn't developing according to schedule. He wasn't arriving at the usual milestones. The baby books like *Dr. Spock's Baby and Child Care* told us, "You know more than you think you do," so trust your instincts. Our instincts and the visible evidence told us plenty. By three months, we knew that Rick should have been able to lift his head and lie comfortably on his stomach. He should have been grasping onto rattles and wiggling his arms and legs. He should have been communicating his needs by crying. He should have been doing all these things, but he wasn't. He could follow us with his eyes and seemed to respond to our voices, but his movements and mannerisms were strange and looked unnatural. By six months, when other babies could sit in a high chair and roll over, Rick still had to lie flat in the same position and was making no attempts to sit up. He couldn't babble like other six-month-olds either.

To help pay for all our medical bills, I started my own masonry business and worked nights and during time off from my military duties. Judy became a stay-at-home mom. It wasn't unusual for a new mother to stay at home with her infant for the first couple of months, but we knew that Judy wouldn't be returning to work. She had to quit her job. Rick needed her at home. So she was left alone with the baby. She found it particularly hard when other mothers would stop by with their babies, wanting her and Rick to go on a walk around the neighborhood. She reached a point where she was scared to go outside or even answer the door for fear she'd have to talk to the other mothers about Rick's issues. She began taking Rick for walks after all the other mothers had gone home for the evening. It was difficult for her and even embarrassing to see mothers pushing their healthy babies in strollers.

Of course, we had the support of our families, but we knew that other people talked and what they were saying was that we were wasting our time on a lost cause. Something was clearly wrong with our baby, be it a mental or physical defect. It was incredibly hard and, without any real answers, we felt we had no safe place to land. Then things got worse. When Rick was around seven months old, we noticed that he was having strange spasms. Judy and I decided that we'd waited long enough. We couldn't keep expecting to wake up with a healthy baby. We had to get some answers so we could understand how to help Rick. We scheduled an appointment with a pediatric specialist in Medford.

After another battery of tests, Rick was eight months old when we finally got an official diagnosis. The news was heartbreaking. The specialist told us that Rick had cerebral palsy, a neurological disorder that permanently affects body movement and muscle coordination. I had no idea what he was talking about and had never heard the words *cerebral palsy* before. Neither had Judy. We were dumbfounded.

It was difficult to accept the news, especially of a disorder neither of us had ever heard of. "Are you sure?" we asked the specialist. He said that he was certain of the diagnosis. Rick had suffered brain damage when oxygen was cut off by his umbilical cord during birth. He had a neurological disorder, which was cerebral palsy. The only thing he couldn't determine was exactly which portion of the brain had been damaged. Rick's motor functions had been seriously affected, but it would take years of development before we would know the extent of the damage to his mental capacity. He even discussed the possibility of a brain operation, exploratory surgery where doctors would intentionally damage another part of Rick's brain in order to counteract the part that was already damaged. There was a fifty-fifty chance Rick would survive the operation, and they weren't exactly sure if it would work. We immediately told them to forget that approach.

One of the biggest hurdles in dealing with and treating cerebral palsy, we were told, is that no two cases are alike. There is no known cure. It can occur at birth, during pregnancy, or even in children up to the age of three. Some babies are only affected physically, while others have mental disabilities or a combination of both. Because there are varying degrees of severity, some people who have cerebral palsy are able to speak well but might walk with a slight limp. Others may talk very slowly or hardly at all. Some walk and even run. Some are wheelchair-bound. Our family doctor in Winchester later explained that his sister's child had cerebral palsy, but he'd had no idea that that was what was wrong with Rick, given the severity of his case in comparison.

The specialist in Medford gave us literature about cerebral palsy, and we met other doctors and therapists who further explained it. It was a lot to take in. Rick was what medical textbooks referred to as a spastic quadriplegic. All four of his limbs had been seriously affected. We were told that this meant he would likely never walk because his muscles were too tight and rigid. Some children with quadriplegia also have tremors or uncontrollable shaking on one side of their body. This explained our son's spasms.

What all this meant for Rick's future was devastating. As we sat listening to doctors and trying to understand what they were saying, I think Judy and I were in shock. It was the only way we could hold back our emotions and keep from breaking down in front of everyone. We asked what we should do next and how to proceed with treatment. Their response suddenly made it clear why we had never heard of cerebral palsy before or even seen a child in a wheelchair. They advised us to put Rick in an institution. Forget about him, the doctors said. Don't visit. Don't think about him. Go on with your life. That's what families in similar situations had done before us.

The doctors reminded us that we were young. We could have other children. There was a one-in-a-million chance of this happening to us again. It was as if they were suggesting we should forget that Rick was ever born. Judy and I may not have known anyone who'd done such a thing—or at least we weren't aware of it—but we knew about institutions. Back then, they were big state schools where people with disabilities were sent. They were rumored to be worse than prison; inmates may have been treated better than the patients in an institution. We heard many sad stories about the children and people who were in these institutions, tales of patients sitting all day in the corner and only being given an occasional bath, babies with dirty diapers left crying in their cribs for hours on end.

Judy and I didn't need a second to confer. Horrified by the suggestion that we deny our son a life with his mother and father, we looked at one another and said, "No way." The doctors tried to convince us that Rick would receive better treatment in an institution and that there was nothing we could do to help him at home. They said our son was nothing more than a vegetable. We didn't care. We couldn't imagine abandoning Rick and living life without him, as if he had never existed. No matter what was wrong with him, Rick was going to remain at home with us.

When we left the doctor's office with Rick in tow, the understanding between Judy and me was that we had no other choice but to raise this baby and try to give him a normal life. On the drive home from Medford, the floodgates opened. We cried the entire way. I kept thinking about what the doctor had told us about Rick's condition and how the experts had called our son a vegetable. It hardly seemed possible that this had happened to our family. We'd wanted answers for so long, but the answers we finally got nearly broke us.

In the twenty minutes it took us to get home, I experienced a gamut of emotions, from anger to sadness to disappointment. If the doctors were right, Rick would never be the athlete I had hoped he might become. He would probably never walk or talk. As he got older, we'd have to buy a wheelchair. I thought about that a lot—a wheelchair for a child, when I'd never even known an adult who had to use one. My dreams of having enough children for our own ball team seemed foolish and out of reach now. Rick would need our undivided attention. I'd already begun crunching numbers, imagining what it was going to cost to be able to provide the kind of care our son would require at home. Judy and I both recognized that this wasn't going to be easy, but the alternative was unimaginable. Through that tearful ride home, we started to plan the rest of our lives around Rick.

Judy and I decided we needed to seek counsel from someone outside the medical community. We called the pastor of our congregational church who had married us and asked if he would come to the house to talk with us. I guess we just wanted to hear that our decision to keep Rick at home was the right one. We felt that it was our only choice, but we needed an unbiased opinion from someone we trusted and who understood such matters from a moral standpoint. We explained to the minister all that we had been through in the past eight months. We told him of the specialist's diagnosis. We showed him our little boy, lying quiet and stiff in his crib. We prayed together and talked.

It was a reassuring meeting—a real turning point in our lives. The minister didn't give us an ultimatum or recommend that we choose one route over another. Instead, without sugarcoating anything, he was straightforward. He said he couldn't predict the future, and as a minister, he didn't know any more about Rick's medical condition than we did. Although he was hesitant to offer advice, he did point out our two choices. Either we could put Rick in a mental institution and forget him, or we could raise him at home the best we could. We'd already been given the first option by doctors and had refused it, so we knew exactly what to do and felt confident in our decision. We would raise and love Rick as we would any child. From then on, there was no discussion of options. We became advocates for our son. We also started meeting with families that included disabled children, and we tried to help one another out by sharing our stories and supporting each other through friendship.

So, despite Rick's obvious special needs, we treated him like a normal baby. Once the doctors recognized that we were going to keep him, they arranged for local housewives and neighbors, who volunteered their time, to come to the house and help us with home therapy—stretching and massaging Rick's arms and legs. As he got a little older, we started taking Rick to Children's Hospital Boston for physical therapy. It was a good hour-and-fifteen-minute trip, and depending on Rick's appointments, we went as often as once a week early on.

Since we'd learned that a lot of children with cerebral palsy had developmental delays or learning disabilities, we were initially worried about what that meant for Rick. But we didn't worry for long. When we talked to him and looked into his eyes, he looked right back at us. We knew he was smart. He was not able to communicate by crying or talking, but he had other ways to let us know what he was feeling or thinking. Judy and I noticed Rick liked to be by the window so he could watch for me when he knew I was coming home from work. When I'd come through the door, he'd smile real big. It was something worth coming home to, just to see the look on his little face and his bright eyes. There was no denying his intelligence.

At Children's Hospital Boston, we finally met a doctor who agreed with us. Dr. Robert Fitzgerald was a psychologist who had been confined to a wheelchair since a bout of polio in his youth. He offered family therapy long before it was common practice. We felt he was the first doctor who really listened to us, and he gave us ideas for making Rick's childhood as normal as possible. He encouraged us to treat Rick as if he were able-bodied, to include him in family activities, and give him the experiences that our friends' babies were having.

As we saw Rick growing and adjusting, Judy and I talked more and more about expanding our family. At this time, Rick was eighteen months old. We really wanted to give him a brother or sister, but we were of course concerned about what might happen. We'd been assured that there was little to no chance of anything like Rick's birth happening again. Still, it made us nervous. I was working two jobs—full-time in the National Guard as well as part-time with my mason business—just to pay for Rick's treatment. Not only would another child with a disability crush us emotionally, we might not survive financially.

Dr. Fitzgerald assured us there was nothing to be afraid of. We were capable of having healthy babies. Our family doctor could monitor the pregnancy and be alert for any problems before they occurred. Dr. Fitzgerald told us that having other children would bring balance to the family and force us to dote less on Rick. Our devotion to our firstborn was apparent, but we were clearly being overly protective because of his disability. Since from the start we'd pushed for others to treat Rick normally, we didn't want to be treating him differently ourselves, whether intentional or not. We decided the time was right to have another child.

It didn't take long for Judy to become pregnant again. On April 17, 1964, our second son, Robert Stanley Hoyt, was born, screaming at the top of his lungs, in the same Winchester hospital where Rick and two other generations of Hoyts had been born. People often ask why we would return to the hospital where we had suffered complications during delivery. Judy and I were never really angry at the doctor. These things simply happen, and you deal with them. We would love Rick just as much as if he had never had his umbilical cord wrapped around his neck.

With the birth of our second child, there were no complications. We had a beautiful, healthy, baby boy who we couldn't wait to take home to meet his big brother.

Chapter 4

Childhood Memories

With two young boys at home, there was never a dull moment. When our family of three had expanded to include little Rob, we learned pretty quickly that having two children under the age of three could sometimes be a handful. Add to that the fact that one child was able-bodied, while the other had special needs. We were determined, though, to follow through on our promise to ourselves that we would raise Rick like any child.

So far, Judy and I had gone the extra mile to ensure that Rick had a normal childhood. When his baby brother came along, our biggest challenge was making sure that Rick didn't feel left out as Rob met certain childhood and developmental milestones. When Rob started crawling and exploring all over the house, I came up with a design for a scooter so Rick could join in. We called it the Creeper, and it was simply a metal basket I'd mounted on wheels. Judy put a pillow in the basket to keep Rick comfortable, and when we laid him on his back on top of the pillow, his stiff little arms and legs were able to kick and propel him forward and backward. He got the hang of it real quick, and the two boys had a good time scooting around together. I also rigged up a therapy ball, something Rick could play with as well. We called this invention the Earth Ball. It was a large, flattened rubber ball that we put Rick on top of. The soft surface allowed him to stretch out and bounce while lying on his back. The bouncing acted as a type of massage, which was therapeutic. But the ball was a plaything, too. He and his little brother played on it together, and if Rick bounced off, they would both just laugh and laugh. It was low to the ground, so there wasn't any danger. The Earth Ball provided hours of entertainment for both boys.

As we adjusted to the idea of having a child with special needs, attitudes improved at home and within the neighborhood, too. I had never seen anything wrong with showing off our baby, but Judy had been concerned. The neighbors knew that we had a baby, and they naturally asked questions. When people outside our family first saw Rick and how he appeared, it was often awkward trying to explain our situation. Judy felt put off by having to answer their questions, as if she had to defend our choice to love our son. I didn't blame the neighbors for being curious. Like us, they had never seen anything like Rick's disability. Most people in our situation were told to shut the windows, draw the shades, and not talk about the child being kept inside. We never felt right about that and knew it was no way to live. Once we began taking Rick everywhere we went, the neighbors came around. They often helped do things around the house, and before long, we were just another happy family in the neighborhood. We developed some really strong friendships.

We wanted Rick to develop as any other child would. Dr. Fitzgerald suggested, as the first step, teaching him the alphabet. Rick always liked to be read to, but we had to find a way to teach him what the letters and words meant. Judy came up with the idea of cutting letters from sandpaper. As Rick was not able to control his hands, we would guide them over the sandpaper letters so he could feel them as well as see them. Judy pasted those letters and signs on just about everything in the house. And it worked. It was obvious that Rick could recognize objects and associate them with letters and words. We'd also bring him pots and pans to feel, so he would know the difference between hot and cold, and learn not to play with hot things. In many ways, it was just like teaching any child. Rick couldn't verbally acknowledge that he understood, but we knew that he did, and we were determined to work toward a communication system that confirmed that.

When Rick was five years old, our family of four turned into a family of five. Our youngest son, Russell, was born on October 17, 1967, with a healthy set of lungs like his brother Rob. Our family was complete, and with three growing boys, it was important that I provide for us. I logged a lot of hours at my masonry business and worked full-time for the Army National Guard on the Nike Hercules missile system. I set my sights on becoming an officer, and by the time Russ was born, I had been accepted to and completed Officers Candidate School and worked my way through the military ranks from second lieutenant to major. The promotions were nice, and the increase in pay grade helped us pay for Rick's medical expenses and physical therapy.

Things were usually tight financially, but we were never short on fun. We made up for what we may have lacked in material possessions by spending quality time together as a family. I had once considered hunting, fishing, and softball my hobbies, but now I spent any time off with my children. Family was the most important use of extra time, and we didn't need a lot of extra money to be happy around one another.

While Rob and Russ were meeting their developmental milestones, our eldest son was meeting his medical milestones. Rick got his first wheelchair fairly early, as soon as he got too big and too old to be carried around. The chair went a long way toward enabling him to get in on the action and at least be sitting upright so he could see the world from that perspective. It also helped with his posture and muscle tension. Rick's body is like cranberry sauce. He has no spinal support. His wheelchairs have always been fitted with forms to keep him from slipping out. Because his muscles are constantly tensing and readjusting, he needs the rigidity. Even now, in a specially fitted wheelchair that's molded to his body, he has to be readjusted often in order to stay comfortable. The chair is his stabilizer. Although we had never before seen an adult in a wheelchair, much less a child, it became a part of our lives, a way to enrich our family and Rick's experience as a member of it. Russ has said that when he was young, he thought every family had a member in a wheelchair. In our lives, that was the norm, and whatever Rick needed, we accepted and attended to as naturally as we would with Rob or Russ. That, after all, had been our goal from the start—to mainstream a child who appeared physically different from other children, but who we knew was as vibrant and active on the inside as his younger brothers were on the outside.

Based on Dr. Fitzgerald's earlier suggestion to take risks and allow our firstborn to participate in the activities that those able-bodied people around him were taking part in, we brought Rick along on family trips or vacations. Rick came everywhere with us, just like the other kids. If we were headed to the store to grab bread or milk, the kids always wanted to come, Rick included. We took the extra time to get his chair in the vehicle and would pile him in with the rest of us. I even took Rick on masonry jobs from time to time. Once I hauled him and his chair up on the roof of a house I was working on so he could see how I was putting together a chimney. Playtime was no different. Rick was right there in the mix. If we went to the beach, Rick went to the beach. We tied fishing line with bait on the end to Rick's finger, and when he would catch something, we would reel it in for him. Rick even played street hockey with his brothers and the neighborhood kids. With a goal stick tied across the front of his wheelchair and one of his brothers steering from behind, he made an excellent goalie.

When Rick was young, we'd gather the entire family to go hiking. I would lead, with Rick draped around my neck in a fireman's hold, and Judy, Rob, and Russ would follow. Sometimes, people just didn't know what to make of us. I'll never forget the time we were all climbing Mt. Monadnock in New Hampshire. Rick and I were in the lead and started climbing the mountain, with Judy and the boys following. A young family passed Rick and me coming from the other direction, and they stared a little as they continued on their way down. When they passed Judy and our two youngest boys, they warned them, "There is a guy carrying his dead son up to the top of the mountain. We think he's going to sacrifice him!" Judy got a kick out that one.

Swimming was an especially favorite pastime for the kids. When Rick was in the water, it was a sight to behold. In Falmouth, we took him to the public pool. If people there hadn't seen us before, we would sometimes catch a few stares and sidelong glances. I guess it did look pretty odd, as we picked Rick up from his wheelchair and tossed him in the water. We would tell Rick to hold his breath while he sunk under the water. I didn't swim then and had never learned how, but Rob and Russ took lessons early on and were excellent swimmers. They never let Rick flounder in the water and would always jump in and float him back to the surface. It's a wonder that other swimmers in the pool didn't think the brothers were intentionally drowning a disabled kid. It was great therapy for Rick. He loved being in the water, and it was a terrific opportunity for him to bond with his younger brothers and learn to trust that they would never fail him. The swimming itself was low-impact exercise that allowed Rick to feel less disabled.

We did, however, have some close calls in the water. The first time I lived in El Paso was before I was married. On my second stint in El Paso, I took my family along as well, and we lived there for a brief time when the boys were still little. Much to my children's delight, our apartment complex had a community pool. While I was down in the shallow end, throwing toddlers Rob and Russ toward the deep end, Rick was relaxing by the edge of the pool. All of a sudden, Rick rolled into the water and quickly sank to the bottom. A fast-acting neighbor rushed into the pool area, dove in, and lifted Rick to safety. Rick came to the surface shooting water from his nose and mouth, and laughing hysterically.

When we moved to Falmouth, Massachusetts, we lived in a house set on a finger of fresh water that fed into the ocean through a causeway. In the summer, the boys would suit up in life jackets and jump into a canoe, paddle to the middle of the estuary, and tip the canoe over—dumping all three of them into the cool salt and freshwater mix. Rob and Russ would swim around, find Rick, and turn him right side up if necessary. Rick would always come up, like the time in the pool, spurting water out of his nose and mouth and laughing. Then his brothers would empty the water out of the canoe, right it, reload, and do it again. I was at work, and Judy always kept a concerned eye on them from the house. While she went about doing housework and other projects, the boys were left to their fun. We tried to give them as much leeway as we thought was safe, but they got away with things when they thought we weren't looking! Miraculously, they survived their childhood antics.

While writing this book, I asked my sons to share some stories from their childhoods. Rob reminded me of one summer when we were living on the Cape, and Judy and I dropped the three boys off at their beloved Grannie's (Judy's mom) house for the evening, while we went out for some time alone. Grannie was very proud of her homegrown tomatoes that she labored over in the sand around her Cape house. How she ever grew them in that sandy soil is beyond me. That summer night, her tomato crop was ready for picking, and she wanted to share her bounty with the boys. Always a little uncomfortable about feeding Rick, Grannie had him covered from head to toe with towels to catch any food that would fall from his backward working tongue. Grannie slipped a sweet slice of tomato into Rick's mouth, and Rick, with a wry smile, shot it right back out at her, missing all the towels and landing it on Grannie's bare feet. The boys loved their Grannie's horrified reaction. Rob said it was one of the best meals he ever had. Rick ate every bite of tomato for the rest of the feast, without spilling a drop.

Rick's sense of humor can catch people off guard. Rob remembers when they were young boys at a speaking engagement at a local college. Rick must have been around fifteen or so. This was during the time that Judy went to local schools and clubs to speak about disability awareness, and sometimes she would take Rick and his brothers along. Rob and Rick were in front of a classroom of college students, while Judy talked about life with the disabled. She stood at the podium with Rick and Rob behind her. Rick had a little fun behind his mom's back. As Judy would explain Rick's inability to use his arms, for instance, he would swing them wildly about. The class, of course, howled with laughter. As the students mingled around Rick at the end of the talk, Rick's spastic hands would conveniently find their way to the rear end or chest of every good-looking girl within striking distance.

Russ shared some great stories, too. One day after school—Rick was around fourteen or fifteen years old at this time—Rick talked his brothers into dressing him up in one of their mother's dresses. Apparently, they also put a bra on him, padded with fruit from the kitchen. They parked Rick in the front hallway so as soon as Judy got home from running errands, she would see how her oldest "daughter" would have looked if things had been different.

Russ recalls (and I remember wanting to wring his neck when it happened) that—at Rick's insistence—he and Rob dug a hole in the woods and placed Rick inside it. Rick was around ten years old at the time. They proceeded to cover the hole with a piece of plywood and cover that with leaves. Then they left his empty wheelchair sitting nearby with a note on it that read,

"Ransom: extend bedtime to 10:00 p.m. and we'll tell you where to dig." You can guess the rest. When Russ and Rob got home shortly before dinnertime and we asked where their brother was, they told us he was waiting for us in the woods. After Judy and I tore out to look for Rick, Russ wisely decided that he and Rob should go to a friend's house before we returned, which is where they stayed until well after dinner.

A central element of all these stories is Rick's enduring and happy spirit. He has always been such a good sport, but would try and pull one over on you for the sake of a good chuckle. He was a child who would much rather laugh than cry and who seemed to have made a conscious decision to do so a long time ago. "He always laughs and smiles at whatever life hands him," Rob told me, "through pain or sadness, through any challenge, every day since day one." Rob has often said that he gets a great deal of inspiration from his big brother and courage to keep going, no matter what. As he wrote to me, "How can anything life hands me be anywhere as challenging as what he faces every day?" I could not have said it better myself.

Chapter 5

Early Education Obstacles

I have always said that Rick has more patience and wherewithal than anyone I have ever known. Even as a little boy, he was a trooper. He adapted wonderfully, considering his disability, and he got along great with his younger brothers and neighborhood kids. Judy and I were regular churchgoers, so we took him to Sunday School and then enrolled him in the church school, a preschool for the young children of those who attended our church. The Sunday School teachers confirmed that Rick was smart, something Judy and I had recognized from the beginning. There was no denying the light in his eyes. Rick knew the alphabet and could identify objects and people. He could signal to us and express his needs. Doctors who said he would never be toilet trained were amazed when we reported that he had been trained earlier than our other two sons. Rick learned to control his bathroom habits at a young age. Everything he did was pretty unbelievable, and other people responded. He was a social butterfly who could light up a room full of people. He had proved that he could play and laugh and learn.

Rick loved being around other people and always had a smile on his face when he got to interact with the other families at Children's Hospital Boston during his physical therapy appointments. The therapy was good for us, too. We met other parents of children with disabilities, who had made the same choice we had to keep their children at home. There were other kids in the group with cerebral palsy, but they weren't as badly afflicted as Rick. Some of them could talk or walk or use their arms. Most who were wheelchair-bound could control their own wheelchairs, unlike Rick. Still, we could compare notes and share ideas about raising a family that included a disabled child. We tried to do things outside of therapy with them as well, whenever fun outings could be arranged so we could all get together. Judy and I even worked on starting a cerebral palsy parents association in our county, so area parents of children with CP could meet and talk about how we could get our disabled children into the public school system. There weren't any people in our immediate community who had children with Rick's disability, but there was at least one family, the Murphys, from Medford, Massachusetts, a few towns away. We got our families together as often as we could to socialize, and we went to each other's kids' birthday parties and such. We knew there had to be others. We didn't want other parents to feel that they were going it alone.

When he was only six years old, Rick was as smart as a whip and a fast learner who possessed incredible patience. He had exceeded everyone's expectations and graduated from the church kindergarten. We were so proud of all that he had accomplished. He was a sweet little boy, though he got into plenty of good mischief with his younger brothers. He had a sly grin and would laugh whenever any of us did something funny. We knew he had a keen sense of humor and was going to turn out to be a real prankster. Rick was right in the middle of everything, just the way he liked it. He was socially active, thanks to church functions, playing with the neighborhood kids, and family outings.

While Rick was attending the private church kindergarten and later being tutored by his mom, we took him to the United Cerebral Palsy training facility in Lawrence, ten or eleven miles away. There we met a supportive occupational therapist, Fay Kimball, who spent a lot of time with Rick and could see what we saw—that Rick was smart and more than capable of understanding and learning. Fay became very instrumental in Rick's progress and was a teacher and therapist who left a positive mark. We know that Rick left a positive impression on her, too. (She would remember our family when an incredible opportunity presented itself.)

With his involvement in all our family activities and his regular visits to Children's Hospital Boston and the cerebral palsy training facility for therapy, both Rick and the rest of the family had a strong grasp on his physical capabilities as well as an understanding of his limitations. We had lived with cerebral palsy for six years, and while we were always learning more about the disorder, we were experts compared to when we had first heard Rick's diagnosis. All of us had come so far. The next step seemed obvious. We knew that our son was ready for the classroom. Because the church didn't provide any schooling beyond kindergarten, Judy and I set about getting Rick enrolled in the first grade in North Reading.

The process was not as simple as we naively assumed it would be. To our dismay, the local school administration refused to allow Rick to attend classes on the grounds that he could not walk, talk, or feed himself. We tried to reason with school officials. Rick was doing well in therapy, and doctors and nurses were amazed by his progress. Our son was intelligent and motivated to learn. He was merely trapped in a body that wouldn't allow him to express his capabilities. The resistance from the public school system was hurtful and troubling. We never wanted Rick to be socially stunted by his challenge, and we sure didn't want him to be educationally stunted as well.

Judy and I refused to be defeated. Judy arranged a hearing with the school board in order to make our case for Rick's attendance in public school. Because of my work, I couldn't attend the hearing. Judy had to go alone and serve as our collective voice. Apparently, things got pretty heated during the hearing, and emotions ran high—on both sides. The most frustrating part, Judy said afterward, was that she felt as if she were getting nowhere. No matter what she said or the evidence of Rick's ability to learn, the school board members wouldn't listen. If it was a matter of concern over his medical situation, she told them, we could arrange for someone to be present in the classroom to care for his physical needs. She pointed out that he was toilet trained and had more control over his body than many kids his age. We had doctors' notes and permission from his primary medical caregivers. We were willing to make any concession to get our son into the classroom—his chance at an education was that important to us—but it seemed those school officials had made up their minds before Judy even presented our case. The answer was still no.

What the members of the school board saw was a severely disabled boy in a wheelchair with two parents in serious denial about his capabilities. They couldn't get past our son's appearance and unfairly judged him because of it. They held fast to their belief that Rick was incapable of communicating and therefore incapable of understanding anything that could be taught to him. Mainstreaming him would do him no good, they told us, and it would only serve as a distraction for the other children. There was no changing their decision.

When I got home from work, Judy was still ticked off about the hearing. After she'd cooled down, we decided that we were determined to make the best of the situation and to somehow change the board members' minds.

Although the school administrators wouldn't allow Rick to sit in the classroom with the other students, they did assign us a home-study program of four hours per week. The only problem was that the program didn't come with a teacher. Judy was left to not only take care of three small boys, but also tutor the only one who was school age. It was hard enough running around after two active toddlers, let alone providing special attention to one child who was disabled. There were times I would come home, and she would tell me she didn't know if she could do it anymore. It was simply too difficult. While she loved being a mother, she had not signed on to serve as full-time educator as well. She felt she was making great strides with Rick, using what she'd learned from the therapists about alternative learning methods and physical interaction, but she didn't feel qualified as a teacher. But Judy persisted, all the while working toward the ultimate goal of getting Rick into the school system. Slowly but surely, with the endorsement of others in the medical field, we began to convince the people in the school system that our son was smart and capable of learning. We were gaining some headway. In the meantime, although Judy and I weren't about to let it be permanent, we were forced to enroll Rick in a school for disabled children.

At that time, the schools for kids with similar conditions were really only nursing facilities. People dropped off their children for the day; that was the extent of it—daycare for the disabled. Rick's school was literally housed in a nursing home, where United Cerebral Palsy rented a section. It was an old brick building in Lawrence that took all kinds of disabled people. Two of the classes for children were divided into "grades" based on ages— four- to eight-year-olds, and nine and up. The program included occupational, physical, and speech therapy. Judy taught swimming lessons to help pay for Rick's therapy. Judy didn't attend classes with Rick; each classroom had a helper to assist the disabled. The teachers in such programs were more like babysitters.

Since the school was for kids with both physical and mental disabilities, you can imagine the kind of education he was getting. It wasn't that those types of programs didn't have merit or that we felt Rick was neglected; it simply wasn't what we knew he needed— the polar opposite. It was akin to the doctors putting glasses on him he was four years old. Rick's brain, just like his eyesight, was fine. Putting him in a classroom with children who were mentally disabled would stunt his growth. Rick really needed one-on-one instruction, but that environment didn't allow it. There was a big room with one teacher and at least a dozen needy children. The teacher did her best, given the situation. It was not as bad as an institution might have been, but we were disappointed and frustrated that an intelligent child was not being given the chance to excel.

One good thing about the school was that it introduced us to other families with disabled children. This enabled us to find extracurricular activities available for kids like Rick—including sports and camps. We were thrilled to sign Rick up for a street hockey league for the disabled. Playing sports made Rick so happy. We could tell by how excited he would get when he knew it was game time and by his bad mood when the game was over and it was time to head home. Rick had inherited my love for sports. He was especially excited about hockey in all forms and was crazy about the Boston Bruins. He had followed their winning (and losing) seasons with rapt attention.

So Rick got to play sports and feel as if he were just another kid. He was competitive and loved to score or, even better, win. He still has a few battle scars to remind him of those early years. Once, when he was around ten years old, at an Easter Seals soccer camp, a counselor accidentally let him slip from her grasp when she got excited about Rick's team scoring a goal. He fell face first out of his chair and onto the hard ground, knocking out his two front teeth. The silver replacements prompted everyone to call him tinsel tooth. Rick loved the attention, and the reason for it. Those replacements didn't stay in for long, as he had a habit of grinding his teeth—the tinsel teeth only lasted for about a year, but he loved them. He claims that injury as his finest and most glorious, since it happened while he was playing sports.

We still couldn't shake our desire to have our son included with everyone else. The rest of the kids his age were headed off to school, boarding the bus every day with their lunch boxes.

All we wanted was the same for Rick. Instead, year after year—for five or six years—Rick would watch from his wheelchair as the neighborhood kids and then his own brothers got on the school bus. He felt left out. Sure, he was going to a school for disabled kids on a part-time basis, but it was not the same as getting on the big yellow bus with all the other kids and going to school all day.

During one of my military school training stints, when we lived in El Paso, Texas, Rick had gone to a special class for the disabled. He got there via public school taxi, which was the closest thing to a school bus he had ever seen. Unfortunately, and unbeknownst to us until an incident occurred, the taxi driver drank. One day, he was in a minor accident while Rick was a passenger. Our son had fallen to the floor of the cab and gotten banged up a little. When the cabbie finally brought Rick home, he was very apologetic to Judy. He kept saying, "He's okay, He's okay. He was just on the floor." But that quickly put a stop to that form of school transportation. From then on, we made other arrangements. We realized that simply transporting Rick to school could involve hurdles. And it seemed to us that the final destination was hardly worth the pain and effort getting there.

All the time Rick attended the schools for the disabled we could tell he wasn't happy in the program. He always looked sad. Even as a kid, Rick always had a smile on his face—he was just generally cheery, but that wasn't the case when he was attending the schools for the disabled. He would even tell us as much. We could ask him yes and no questions, and he would respond. When we asked if he was happy at school, he would shake his head no. While the staff at the schools for the disabled were not unkind to him, his mind was not being stimulated. He was just another kid in a wheelchair, a child who couldn't walk or talk and therefore only needed to be pushed about from one room to the next.

Now, it seems so obvious that you don't make assumptions about a person's mental capacity simply because he cannot stand upright or voice what he's thinking. Neither the wheelchair nor Rick's inability to talk bothered or stopped us. The wheelchair had become such an extension of Rick that it was like a part of him. Rick may not have been able to vocalize his thoughts, but we had learned to interpret his expressions and had taken the time to teach him language skills, just as you would any child. However, in the late 1960s and early 1970s, public attitudes hadn't quite caught up with the fact that a growing number of the population was disabled. They were just hidden away. Rick, without knowing or perhaps even wanting to be, was a pioneer in uncharted territory. As parents, we knew that he deserved the opportunities he was being denied. Despite our disappointments, we didn't give up. We knew there had to be a solution, if only we could prove that our child was capable of communicating. That was the ticket to getting our son the education we longed for him to have. We were determined to somehow make it happen. We were in it for the long haul. It would take several years—until Rick turned twelve—a team of Tufts engineers, a computer, and legislation before Rick was finally admitted to a public school.

Chapter 6

Tufts University

At eight years old, Rick was still unable to communicate vocally. Due to the way his muscles constantly tensed, writing and sign language were not possibilities either. We had long since learned how to interpret our son's smiles and nods, his "yes" and "no" head shakes, but as good as everyone in the family was about figuring out what Rick needed, we were still only making educated guesses. Sometimes, we were wrong or it took an awfully long time to stumble on what was right. Rick's inability to communicate was keeping him out of the public schools and, we feared, was responsible for him falling behind.

After several years of wondering if we would ever be able to prove Rick's mental capabilities and find a way for him to take part in a conversation, we were suddenly given reason to hope. During one of Rick's therapy visits in Lawrence, we were introduced to Dr. William Crochetiere, who was then the chairman of the engineering department at Tufts University in Medford, Massachusetts, along with a group of four or five graduate students in the computer engineering program. Fay Kimball, Rick's early champion and occupational therapist, had invited them to see what kinds of needs the training facility had. She had heard about their work with other disabled people and the kinds of innovations they had made with advanced communications for mostly older adults. She hoped to forge a partnership between the programs. She also wanted them to meet us on the off-chance they might be able to help Rick. After facing so much rejection, however, we tried to remain cautiously hopeful.

When the doctor and his students met Rick for the first time, they were polite but skeptical. It seemed we were going to get the same response we had received from the medical community—this child is a lost cause. Then one of the grad students asked the question I could tell they all wanted to ask: "How do you know your son is smart?" Desperate for them not to write us off, Judy told them the first thing that came to her mind. "Go ahead and tell him a joke," she said. I will never forget the moment when Dr. Crochetiere kneeled down by our son's wheelchair and did exactly that. Though I can no longer remember the joke, whatever the doctor said was funny to Rick. When Dr. Crochetiere delivered the punch line, Rick immediately threw his head back laughing, just as we knew he would.

As an uncommunicative and severely disabled child, Rick's sense of humor has been a lifesaver in a lot of tense moments. There were plenty of times when we thought our situation was too difficult and the challenges insurmountable; then one of us would do something funny, and Rick would burst out laughing. It would break the tension at precisely the time we needed it and make us realize that the difficulties we faced weren't roadblocks, merely speed bumps on this road we call life. Rick was still cracking up when Judy and I looked around the room and realized we were the only ones laughing. The engineers just sat in amazement. After that, they were all on board. They were convinced that, given the right tools, Rick would be able to communicate. They eagerly returned to their university lab to begin to design a computerized communication device. If only it had been as easy to get Rick into public school as it had been to convince a group of engineers to build us a computer. Strangers, most of them young students, had agreed to spend their valuable time and resources developing a device that had the power to change my family's future. That was one of the happiest days our family had ever spent at the cerebral palsy training facility.

The device, of course, had to be created, and that took time. Spearheading the project was Rick Foulds, an eager, hardworking, young graduate student who completely immersed himself in the project. The work he was doing often went well beyond my understanding. He was convinced he could create a communication device to help not just my son, but others who were unable to vocalize or express their thoughts. His confidence proved reliable.

After six weeks, after hundreds of hours logged sketching and researching and building, Foulds and the other students—who, in addition to working on the computer were completing their other coursework and teaching responsibilities—came up with the first version of their communicator. Mind you, this was in 1970, when few people had computers or knew anything about them. What the team came up with was a bulky machine, though portable, and consisted of a display monitor with rows of letters, numbers, and symbols. In a process they called scanning, the machine worked by flashing lights in a sequence along the panel, pausing briefly on each letter, number, or symbol. By simply clicking a switch, whoever was operating the machine could select the letter, number, or symbol he wished to display on the screen. In Rick's case, he would be able to activate the switch and create sentences by pressing his head against a metal bar attached to the side of his wheelchair and connected to the computerized system. Foulds and his fellow students called the contraption the Tufts Interactive Communicator (TIC, for short). In our household, we immediately took to calling it the Hope Machine because that is what it brought us: hope.

In the first trial runs, we saw a little success. However, because of the nature of the machine and how it operated, we were limited by what we could do with it. Rick learned how to use the head switch to locate letters, but the equipment was too cumbersome and too slow for him to communicate with us in complete sentences. Despite initial setbacks, we were thrilled by the possibilities. The team, sure that they were on to something, decided to return to the drawing board to redesign the machine and create a smaller version, one that was more trustworthy and with an improved switch activator. The only stumbling block was that the newer version was going to cost a lot of money, $5,000 if we wanted it done right. In the early 1970s, $5,000 was a lot, and we were already on a very tight budget. We were lucky that the first version of the communicator had been free to us, since the inventive and dedicated grad students had used surplus materials and had not charged for their labor. As appreciative as we were of what they had already done for our family, we weren't about to fall short of the goal only because we were unable to afford a better model.

Word got out pretty quickly about what we were doing to try to improve Rick's quality of life. Everyone was excited for us and the possibility that our son might one day be able to communicate. Since people seemed interested, we wanted to show them the machine and what it would mean for us to be able to fund the development of an even better version. With the help of some of the grad students, we held demonstrations of the TIC at churches and other local groups, which helped us to garner individual donations. Our church sponsored a crafts fair. The area kids put on a little carnival bazaar and raised $40 or $50. Friends and neighbors stepped up to help, and mothers got together on weekends and had bake sales, which were so popular that we made $300 or $400 from cakes and brownies alone. Then there was the big dinner-dance our family threw, where we earned most of the money. We rented out a hall where we could host it and provided dinner and held a dance afterward. Finally, after months and months of fund-raising and tremendous support from the community, we had raised $5,000—exactly the amount the engineers would need to resume work.

Before too long, a second version of the communicator was ready. That one was a lot lighter than the previous version, and had a switch that was knee- instead of head-activated. Rick worked with that TIC for more than a year, and he seemed to get a better handle on navigating the letters and controlling the switch. But ultimately it did not work, as Rick couldn't control his knee movements that well, so the knee switch was not that effective for him. It wasn't exactly what the engineers had envisioned for the final version. They were determined to keep at it until they got it exactly right.

By late winter of 1974, Foulds called to say that the Tufts team had finished work on the TIC. Our Hope Machine had been completed and was ready for its trial run. The third installment of the TIC was a big improvement over the first two and actually printed out what Rick was typing. It also had a head switch instead of a knee switch, since Rick was able to control his head movements more than his knee movements. Rick was barely twelve years old when Foulds and the other students brought the TIC to our home for its debut.

We had invited Rick's therapists, our friends, neighbors, and supporters to see the third version. Foulds switched on the TIC, and the rows of letters lit up. The room fell silent, and all we could hear was the hum of the computer. Foulds encouraged our son to go ahead and try to talk to us. With Rick in place and the crowd gathered behind him, everyone peered forward, trying to guess what his first words would be. I just knew they would be "Hi, Dad." Judy was convinced he would type "Hi, Mom." His brothers thought they might be Rick's first topic of conversation. Maybe he would tell us he loved us, or maybe it would be a simple "Thank you."

Rick began to type, tapping with the side of his head. A *G* and then an *O* appeared on the screen. What in the world, I thought? For a second, I worried that our efforts had been in vain. Though I knew Rick understood us, maybe he didn't understand how to translate what he'd been taught into words and sentences. Rick tapped some more. A *B* then an *R* then a *U* appeared. The light beam flashed over the letters. Rick concentrated and hit the switch. The U was followed with an *I - N - S*. "Gobruins?" someone asked. There was the briefest of pauses. "Go, Bruins!" I hollered, practically jumping up and down. Rick nodded and smiled, pleased with himself. I couldn't quit shaking my head and laughing. There wasn't a dry eye in that house. My heart swelled. I was so proud of my son at that moment. Not only had we finally proved that Rick was capable of communicating, but he really did love sports. That season, the Boston Bruins were in the Stanley Cup Finals. Of course, we'd all been watching. Rick had been silently cheering for them, too. He was his father's son, all right.

In those two little words, "Go Bruins," we were all victorious. Rick had gained independence and proved both his intelligence and sense of humor. He told me later that he could handle not being able to walk or use his arms, but the inability to communicate was what bothered him most. Judy and I felt vindicated in a pursuit that had lasted over a decade. We knew we now had the proof, the hard evidence, that would gain Rick entry into schools and programs he had long been denied.

The changes that came over our family and community were incredible, all because of a computer. The boys were finally able to talk and, as children will do, sometimes argue with one another. Rob and Russ learned what a quick wit their brother was, and they had some pretty amusing conversations. They now had a big brother who, they would soon learn, could play that older brother role and tell them what to do.

And it was a victory for the hardworking team of Tufts engineers. They had created a one-of-a-kind machine that gave life back to a boy who had once been labeled a vegetable. Their success with Rick's TIC impressed the academic, research, and medical communities so much that it led to the creation of a biomedical engineering center at the Tufts Medical Center in Boston. Foulds received his PhD from Tufts and was named director of the center. Rick's computer was the first of many such projects that would be funded to help the disabled.

The test versions of the TIC were slow, only allowing for a couple words per minute. Even the final product took hours of practice. Because Rick was still catching up on spelling and grammar, Russ thought there was no reason he couldn't teach Rick what he was learning in school. So Russ came up with a way to figure out what Rick was thinking without using the computer. He created what we came to call the Russell Method. Using the same concept of the TIC, he divided the alphabet into five blocks, each beginning with a vowel. It was a lot like the game "Twenty Questions." The person asking Rick something would first figure out in which block of the alphabet the word Rick was looking for started with and then would go through the rest of the word's letters quickly until Rick confirmed the right one by nodding his head. In this way, the boys could surpass the computer's capabilities and guess complete words and sentences in much less time, often before Rick had spelled out entire words. It was so effective and efficient that later on, even his personal care assistants (PCAs) used it. Despite the technological advances made with Rick's computerized communicator, we still use the Russell Method in a pinch. It works great when Rick is without his computer.

But it was the Hope Machine that really brought us hope for our son's future. For the first time, we began to imagine a full life for Rick, one that afforded him opportunities we'd never have imagined, including the chance to attend school. We knew that Rick's computer proved our argument that our child was capable of learning and communicating. As technology and the TIC versions improved over the years, so did our attitudes—and our drive to make good on our goals. We were bound and determined to get Rick into public school.

Chapter 7

Chapter 766

With Rick chatting up a storm on the TIC, or Hope Machine, and our family adjusting to the busy life with three talkative and active kids, you would think we wouldn't have had time for causes and political pursuits. However, with the changes the Hope Machine had brought to our lives, Judy was more set than ever on getting Rick into public school. She wasn't about to sit back and let any chance at improving our son's future pass her by. She had not only stepped up her ongoing campaign with the local schools, she had also gone statewide and began frequenting legislative sessions and having heated discussions with

Massachusetts politicians about the injustice disabled children in our state were forced to endure. She joined advocacy groups and attended frequent policy meetings. She was right there in the thick of it and it paid off. Because of Judy's efforts, as well as the work of families with disabled children across the state of Massachusetts, Governor Francis Sargent had signed the Bartley-Daly Act, more commonly known as Chapter 766 a couple years earlier, on July 12, 1972. It was the very first comprehensive special education reform law in the country.

Chapter 766 was drawn up with the intention of ensuring that every child between the ages of three and twenty-one who has special needs receives a free public school education—without fear of isolation from the regular student population. In order to identify any concerns about learning abilities, the law requires that local schools screen all children (beginning at age three) for disabilities. The expectation was that both parents and the schools would be informed about any developmental delays and the best way to handle them. Parents could then receive what's called an Individualized Educational Plan (IEP) for their child, and the child's education could move forward from there. Judy and I were thrilled to see the law passed, but realized that it might not be an immediate fix. If I knew anything about politics, I knew that passing a law didn't always translate into abiding by the law. These things take time, no matter how anxious we were for it happen. Just because the bill was passed in 1972, that did not mean it automatically allowed all disabled kids into every school in Massachusetts. Parents of disabled children still had to appeal to their respective school districts, and each child was accepted to school on an individual basis. So even though Rick was making excellent use of his TIC and showing everyone exactly what he was capable of, by 1974 Judy was still fighting to get him into school.

In spite of our nervousness, waiting around for what was next, everything seemed to be progressing smoothly. Our hectic lives were filled with promise. My job seemed to be going well, Rick was doing great, and the boys were growing like weeds. Then the military stepped in. I had completed my training in El Paso and was in the process of switching from the Army National Guard to the Air National Guard when I was assigned to Otis Air Force Base on Cape Cod. At that time, there were nuclear weapons coming to Otis, and the Air Force was ramping up security. Since my experience was in nuclear weaponry, I guess I looked like an ideal candidate. They needed a large security police force, and I was named the chief of security police. The new job meant that we had to make yet another move, this time to Falmouth. I loved the Cape Cod area and always wanted to live there, so I was excited about the move. It was exactly where I wanted to be at that time of my life. With the guarantee that this job would last at least ten years, I took our life savings and bought our dream home—a big, beautiful, five-bedroom, three-bath house, right on the water—and we made preparations for a long future in Falmouth.

A new home meant a new school for Rick—always a struggle. While I was busy with my new job, Judy was left to handle all the schooling issues. Once again Rick was dumped into a class with all kinds of people with a variety of disabilities. Despite the new legislation, it seemed that nothing had changed in the school district. Fortunately, Rick's teacher, Ms. Laurel Brown, immediately recognized Rick's intelligence and talked to a third-grade math teacher and a fifth-grade science teacher about having him join their classes. They agreed. It was a start, at least. Judy and Ms. Brown were also fighting with the school therapist. Both kept saying that they believed Rick could handle being in a regular class. Judy pointed to the recent change in law that she had helped push through. She had Rick demonstrate what he could do with his TIC. Finally, they compromised and Rick was provided an IEP.

As we got settled into Falmouth and eased into our usual routine, Judy started to think that a degree in education might help her fight to improve the situation for disabled children in the education system. Before she could do anything, though, our long-term plans for Falmouth quickly came to a screeching halt.

By 1975, less than a year after we had uprooted our lives and moved to Falmouth, the military realized it no longer had a need to store nuclear weaponry. So my position at Otis Air Force Base was terminated. I was offered one of two options—a job in Boston or one in western Massachusetts. I chose the job in Westfield, a two-and-a-half hour drive inland. We hated to move because we loved our location across the water from Martha's Vineyard and our beautiful home we had worked so hard for. Judy had felt she was making headway with the public schools there. But the Air National Guard didn't give me other options. If I wanted a job, we had to sell the house and move to Westfield.

The move turned out to be a real blessing—a new start in a new town. As soon as we got settled, Judy enrolled at the University of Massachusetts in Amherst in order to work on an education degree. She took as many classes as her hectic schedule with the boys would allow. It was nearly thirty miles from Westfield to Amherst.

That summer, we looked into the public school options, consulting with doctors, politicians, and lawyers. We told our story and our plans for the future to anyone who would listen. I continued to work as many jobs as I could, trying to provide for us while at the same time balancing work and time at home with the family. It was a busy, busy period in our lives, but we were very happy. It had been a long road to get as far as we had, and we only had one more step to reach our ultimate goal. Massachusetts had begun implementing Chapter 766 during the 1974–1975 school year, so we knew the chances were good that Rick could finally attend public school. We remained hopeful.

Before the start of the 1975–1976 school year, Judy and I packed up Rick and his TIC and headed for the Westfield Elementary School, where Rob and Russ were already enrolled. We had called ahead, and they were expecting us. (By then, the Hoyt name was notorious throughout Massachusetts; Judy had talked to so many educators and legislators that it was hard to keep track of them all.)

When we arrived at the school, the principal and several teachers led us inside for a conference. After talking as a group for a few minutes, the school staff took Rick into a classroom and left Judy and me waiting outside the door. Inside, we could hear them asking our son questions. Then we could hear him responding with his computer. It didn't take long, certainly not as long as I had expected, for them to decide that Rick was ready for public school. He had answered their questions correctly, so they had no choice but to admit that Rick was capable of learning and communicating and that he had a right to be in the classroom with other able-minded and able-bodied children.

A few days before school started, Judy took Rick and his brothers to the school superintendent's office. She had Rick's IEP, which said he should be fully integrated into regular classes, as well as the go-ahead from the Westfield Elementary School administration. She also had the law on her side. Chapter 766 clearly allowed for not just Rick, but countless others in the same condition to attend public school. Judy demanded that our eldest son be accepted. All the superintendent needed was a few days to sort through the paperwork. And just like that, Rick was allowed to enter the fifth grade.

Finally, in 1975, our disabled son, who doctors had told us would never amount to anything more than a vegetable, was admitted to a public school. Our long struggle to mainstream Rick in the public school system was finally over. The Hope Machine had done wonders toward proving his intelligence. The Westfield Elementary School administration had been forced to allow him to enter the halls of the school like any other child.

We had achieved our goal, but Judy wasn't through yet. She had a taste for politics and had seen how persistence and determination really could pay off. First, she recruited other parents and volunteers to help other disabled children who, like Rick, were now able to attend regular classes. This took a burden off both the parents and the school, knowing that the disabled children were not only learning but doing so in a safe and comfortable environment.

The next year, Judy volunteered and became very active in the Association for Human Services (ASHS) in Westfield, an organization that she actually started and organized (though it has since dissolved). At ASHS, she was put in charge of recreational programs for the disabled. She started Kamp for Kids, a summer program for both disabled and able-bodied youth, through age twenty-one. Kamp for Kids had all sorts of activities—from camping and fishing to swimming and other sports—all based on Judy's idea that the disabled and the able-bodied should be integrated rather than kept apart. Judy intended it to be a place that could be enjoyed by families, where no one felt left out because of a disability. All three of our sons loved participating in the program every summer and formed some lasting friendships with the other children who went.

Meanwhile, Judy became involved with Easter Seals organization and got the Westfield High School to open its swimming pool to disabled children. We'd seen how wonderful swimming had been for Rick, so it was great that the school would offer that kind of therapy to other students with disabilities. With our sons thriving in both school and after-school activities and the programs she'd developed such a success, Judy quickly finished her undergraduate degree and decided to continue on in the graduate program at the University of Massachusetts, pursuing a degree in special education.

In just a few short years, amazing changes had come over our family. I was happy to see all three children in public school, enjoying the advantages of education. I knew how hard Judy had worked to get Rick there. It had been her passion, and I was glad that she had had a way to connect with him. In many ways, I longed for that kind of connection with my son. I spent as much time with Rick—as much time with all my boys—as my work would allow. Sometimes work provided me the opportunity to help out in unexpected ways. With Kamp for Kids, for instance, I could provide camping equipment and tents, thanks to the supplies available to me at the National Guard. I coached the boys in Little League baseball in the summer. But I couldn't always be there for everything. Though our struggles may have eased over the years, our expenses hadn't gone away.

It was my job to make sure we could continue living comfortably. Often, that meant my one-on-one time, especially with Rick, was limited.

I kept thinking there had to be a better way, some activity that we could do together, father and son, that would let Rick know how much I cared about him and how proud I was of all he had achieved. For the moment, though, there was school, and that was pretty special.

Chapter 8

Jimmy Banacos Charity Race

No one in our family was surprised when Rick excelled in public school. We had fought so hard to get him in that we knew if he only had the chance to be around the other able-bodied and able-minded children, he'd become a totally different child who felt included and could imagine a future in which anything was possible.

Rick loved school. He took to it like a fish to water. We knew he'd have no trouble with the academic aspect. Of course, he had his moments, just like his brothers or any kid, when he didn't feel like doing his homework or would rather be outside playing or goofing around, instead of indoors focusing on his studies. Studying was a struggle for Rick, simply because it took him longer to do any written work or formulate responses than it would a child who could use his arms or could speak. He had to have tutors and scribes and rarely did any school-related activity without an aide to help. But he'll tell you that it was worth the extra effort. Rick hardly ever complained, because the positive benefits of being enrolled in public school far outweighed the disadvantages. He was popular, and the kids all seemed to accept him. I know that made him feel good. Rick got to be a normal kid like any other. For us, that simple luxury meant the world.

When Rick started seventh grade at Westfield Middle School, he was keeping up with his classmates in every arena—except, admittedly, the physical. He enjoyed playing on the disabled youth sports teams and would swim with his friends from cerebral palsy classes. He was a sports nut like his dad and rarely missed one of his brothers' games. At school, though, physical education was another matter. When it was time for the other kids to go to the gym and shoot hoops, run laps, or play dodgeball, Rick's aid wheeled him into the library. He would use that time to study, get caught up on his homework, or simply wait until it was time to go back to the regular classroom. But that exclusion didn't last long.

The gym teacher, Steve Sartori, saw that there was a kid on his roster who wasn't showing up for P.E., and he went to investigate. He had no idea who Rick was or that he was disabled; he only knew that someone wasn't showing up for class. He called us to let us know that our son had been skipping class. Judy had to keep from laughing as the gym teacher began to lecture her on truancy. She quickly explained the situation and told Coach Sartori that, given Rick's physical challenges, we didn't see a way for him to be involved in P.E. with the other kids. We were lucky he had been admitted to school at all. Sartori hardly skipped a beat when he told Judy that a disability was not an excuse to cut class. He gave her two options: either Rick could come to P.E. or she could come to P.E. for him. Judy wasn't about to turn down an offer of normalcy for Rick—or suit up for gym class herself. So the next day, Rick's aid wheeled him into the gymnasium instead of the library. The rest, as they say, is history.

Sartori immediately took a liking to Rick and was really good with him. He put Rick right in the middle of all the P.E. class activities, joining in with the rest of the kids. He even developed new activities geared especially for our son, things that he could do to participate but that the other kids might enjoy as well. Rick loved it. He really respected his coach, and they developed a special bond. Sartori served as both mentor and friend. Rick would come home from school in the evening and all he wanted to talk about on his TIC was what he got to do in gym class. We were thrilled that Rick was included and accepted. To see him so happy made all our efforts to get him in school worth it.

One evening, Sartori, who also coached for the Westfield State College basketball team, asked if it would be okay for him to take Rick to one of the games. He'd go as the coach's special guest, with some of his other classmates. They'd even get to meet the cheer-leaders, a bonus the coach and Judy and I knew would delight Rick, who at fifteen had clearly developed an interest in girls. We were happy to let Rick attend the game. By then, Sartori seemed like a member of the family. Rick could barely contain his excitement when we told him that he could go. Not that he'd have accepted no for an answer. He later claimed that he would have crawled all the way if he had had to. He was going to that game.

I've often wondered what would have happened if, for whatever reason, Rick hadn't attended that college basketball game with Sartori. That game changed our lives and brought my relationship with Rick to a whole new level. Until that day, I don't think I had ever seen Rick more excited to go somewhere. We loaded him into the coach's van, and they took off for Westfield State College. They wanted to get to the game an hour early in order for Rick to visit with the players in the locker room and watch the team practice.

Judy and I busied ourselves at home that evening, knowing that Rick was having a good time but also feeling a little nervous about his first big outing away from home without us. That day felt special in many ways. We felt that our little boy was maturing into a young man, something made all the more evident by the fact that for so long, so many people had told us Rick would never grow up. My only regret about Rick maturing so fast—before our very eyes—was that I didn't always get to spend as much time with him as I would have liked, doing the kinds of things I did with his younger brothers. I think he understood that we had to make certain concessions because of his disability and that our father-son activities sometimes had to be different from the ones his brothers got to experience with me. But I've always regretted that it took Rick and me as long as it did to find a special activity that we could share. Fortunately for us, the basketball game brought the perfect activity to our attention.

When Sartori pulled into the driveway that night after the game, Rick was sitting in the backseat, grinning from ear to ear. When we got back in the house, he immediately wanted to be hooked up to his computer. He began typing away while the coach filled us in on the game. They'd had a great time, the coach said, and got to meet the players and cheerleaders. Rick had a few autographs to commemorate the event. The trip was so successful that Sartori thought they might have to make it a regular outing. The entire time that the coach was describing the evening's events, Rick was tapping on his headrest, getting his thoughts to the screen. When he had finished, I took a look at what he was so excited to tell me. He had written something about a charity race for someone named Doogie. While Rick continued typing, I asked Sartori what my son was talking about.

Jimmy Banacos, or "Doogie" as he was known to his friends, had been an athlete at Westfield State. Nineteen-year-old Jimmy was an active college student, a star in WSC intramurals, and an important member of the track and lacrosse teams. All that changed one spring day in 1977, when during a lacrosse game, he collided with another player. Jimmy broke his neck and became paralyzed from the neck down. The former athlete was now a quadriplegic. Rick knew about Jimmy because when Sartori wheeled my son into the gym for the basketball game, they were greeted by posters for a charity event to be held in Jimmy's honor. "Run for Doogie," the poster had exclaimed. Sartori knew Jimmy and said what a shame it was that all that talent had been lost. It had obviously been a difficult blow for the college community.

Later, during halftime, one of the cheerleaders made an announcement about the event over the PA system. The next Saturday, the college would be sponsoring a five-mile race to raise money to help pay Jimmy's medical bills. Knowing my son like I do, I began to put two and two together. Just as I was realizing that he wanted to somehow help out with the event, Rick finished typing the words he'd been working on. He had written that he wanted to run in the race. That was fine with me, I told him, as long as Sartori was up for it. Rick began furiously typing again. When

I read what he wrote, my heart sank a little but at the same time swelled with pride. My son didn't want to enter the race with his gym coach. He wanted to enter it with me.

I immediately promised Rick that we would do it. We would enter the race and help this boy, who I knew Rick could relate to. I was so proud of him for wanting to help someone else in a similar situation, someone confined to a body that didn't work right and, no doubt, someone with a family like ours, facing hefty medical bills. I was proud to see that Rick could sympathize. Though I agreed to the race on the spot, later that night I was lying awake for a long time, worrying about how the two of us could ever manage to finish a race. You have to remember that, in addition to Rick being a wheelchair-bound, spastic quadriplegic, I was thirty-seven years old. About the only exercise I got was an occasional jog around the neighborhood or a pickup hockey game if I had the time. A runner I was not.

In the days leading up to the race, I had to buy a pair of running shoes because I didn't own any. I'm not sure what I thought we'd do about Rick's wheelchair. I guess I figured we'd manage somehow. At that time, in 1977, Rick's chair looked something like a cross between a shopping cart and a high chair. It was precision-made to conform to Rick's body, but pretty unwieldy. Clearly, it was not made for running or for being pushed by a runner. Ultimately, though, I had to forget any obstacles and do this for my son. I was out of shape and long past my athletic days, but Rick was born with the heart of an athlete. He wanted to make a difference, and I couldn't deny him that chance. I wouldn't know until after that first race was over, but we had finally discovered the special activity that Rick and I could do together. It would strengthen our relationship in ways that nothing has topped since.

Chapter 9

Day of the First Race

Jimmy Banacos Day, October 22, 1977, was a beautiful fall day in Massachusetts. The benefit road race was set to begin first thing that morning. Our whole family woke up early that Saturday, excited to start the day and take part in the festivities. We went about our usual routine, but everything we did seemed different somehow, as if we sensed that the charity race was the start of something special for our family, the first day of the rest of our lives. Little did we know how true that feeling would turn out to be.

We had breakfast—I ate light, not knowing how my stomach was going to handle pounding the pavement for five miles. We fed

Rick as usual, knowing he was going to need the energy, probably even more than I would. I was admittedly nervous about how he would handle being pushed in the chair for that long, with me running behind him, on what might not be the smoothest of surfaces. Would we have to stop? Would he be able to last the entire race without tiring out? Would I? Pushing those thoughts aside, I concentrated on getting dressed and ready for the big day. I tied my new sneakers. Back then, I didn't know the difference between regular old sneakers and running shoes and had bought a pair on sale without care for fit or style. I pulled on a pair of shorts and a sleeveless T-shirt. The sun was already peeking through the fall foliage, and the local weather prediction was for highs in the upper sixties. I knew I would get hot running, but that early in the morning, it was a little chilly out, so we dressed Rick in a zip-up sweat suit and brought a blanket to drape over his lap. We filled water bottles. The younger boys found their football to toss around in case they got bored. Then we loaded everyone in the van and took off for the race.

The parking lot of the Westfield State College gym was buzzing with people. Runners were pinning numbers to their chests, and their supporters were wishing them well and beginning to gather along the route that local police officers had cordoned off for the race and the parade to be held afterward. Cheerleaders swished their pom-poms, and friends of Jimmy Banacos held up encouraging signs. As far as I could tell, Rick's was the only wheelchair in sight. We made our way through the crowd to find Coach Sartori, who had planned to meet us and had already helped us preregister. We found him near the check-in desk, where he introduced us to his wife, who had a camera hanging around her neck to document the event. The coach handed us our participant number, a double zero, which gave us all a laugh. Russ and Rob gave their big brother a good ribbing, joking about how the number reflected both our chances and the gap from Rick's two missing front teeth. Rick's uncontrollable habit of grinding his teeth had by then made his silver replacements mere specks on his gums. It was quite a sight. The ribbing was all in good fun. We were proud to wear the double zero, the first number of all the race participants. Instead of pinning the number to my shirt, I taped it, facing out, to the top frame of Rick's wheelchair, so everyone would know we were a team.

As we worked through the crowd to the starting line, I could feel people staring and wondering what on earth we were planning to do. Event organizers hadn't given us any trouble about participating, largely because Sartori had already explained to the race director that although Rick was wheelchair-bound, there wasn't any harm in letting him take part. Sartori made it clear how important the race was to Rick and how much he wanted to participate. We were paid participants, just like all the other runners. We had no trouble signing up. But I could tell by the looks on people's faces that they didn't reckon on us making it very far along the route. As the starting time loomed, I steeled myself against the possibility that this race might be too much to handle, a challenge that we weren't yet ready for. "Are you planning on running all five miles?" Mrs. Sartori asked before we said our goodbyes and took our place at the starting line. "You bet," I told her. Judy laughed and said that I might make it as far as the first corner before I turned back. "Oh we'll run the whole race. Rick won't want to stop at the corner," I said. "Neither will I." I can tell you now that I was putting up a brave front. In truth, I had no idea how far we'd make it, but I was determined not to quit.

As I stood at the starting line of my first race, poised behind my son's wheelchair, with the morning sun's rays just beginning to warm the handles of his chair, I felt good. It took me back to my high school days and the feeling I would get right before the start of a football game. I'd be huddled with my teammates in the football locker room, and we could hear the roar outside and the cheerleaders out on the field revving up the crowd that was waiting for us to run out on the field. But that was over twenty years and no doubt as many pounds ago. I was nowhere near the athlete I had once thought I was.

I looked around at the thirty or so other runners standing next to us at the starting line. All were slim and lean-muscled, looking like they were in it to win. I suddenly felt the years of inactivity weighing on me. I also felt worried for my son—did he really know what he was getting into? He'd been insistent all week leading up to the race, but I had to know that in that moment, this was what he really wanted. I knelt down in front of his wheelchair and asked Rick if he was certain he wanted to run the race. I said that we could go as far as he wanted. Or not run at all. It was not too late to back out. No one was expecting anything. Rick shook his head no and indicated that he wanted to go ahead. He couldn't stop smiling as he watched his classmates and teachers standing in the supporting line. I knew then that I wasn't going to let him down. This was something he needed to do, and I needed to do it for him. I straightened up, stretched my legs behind me, and braced myself for the run. An announcer counted down over a megaphone, and we were off. Or, more accurately, the thirty other runners in the race were off ahead of us. But we were moving, too.

I had known that running behind a standard wheelchair was not going to be easy. Simply pushing it and walking behind it

Above left: Rick as a child, 1964. Above right: Rick in his first wheelchair, 1965. *(Dick Hoyt)*

Dick and Rick enjoying the ocean at Cape Cod, 1964. *(Arline Garlington)*

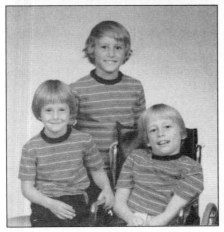

Rick with his brothers Russ (left) and Rob (center), 1971. *(Dick Hoyt)*

Rick with his TIC (Tufts Interactive Communicator) at school, with classmate Wendy LaPlante Bicknell and brother Russell. *(Dick Hoyt)*

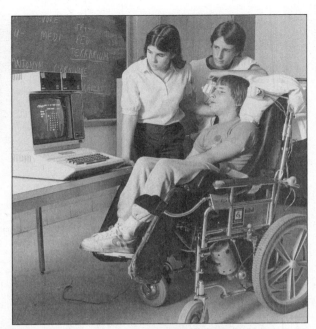

Team Hoyt finishing their first Boston Marathon, April 1981. *(R.S.H.)*

Team Hoyt's first race, Westfield, Massachusetts, 1977. *(Pamela Sartori)*

Marine Corps Marathon,
Washington D.C., 1987.
(R.S.H.)

Rick's graduation
day from Boston
University, 1993.
(Dick Hoyt)

Family photo at Disney World, October 2002. Back row, from left: Troy, Cameron, Dick, Rob, Jayme, Russell. Front row, from left: Rick, Ryan (in carriage), Lisa. *(Barbara Enos)*

Aloha! The family in Hawaii for the 2003 Ironman Competition. Back row, from left: Russell, Dick, Rob. Rick in front. *(Lisa Hoyt)*

Rick, Dick, and girlfriend Kathy Boyer taking part in the Ironman Parade of Nations in Kona, Hawaii, October 2005. *(Joe Widner)*

Dick and Rick with Dick's grandsons Troy and Ryan at an Easter Seals dinner, April 2006. *(Russell Hoyt)*

Dick and Rick on the bike portion of the 2007 Ford Ironman World Championship 70.3 Triathlon in Clearwater, Florida, November 2007. *(Michael Guarino)*

Guy Morse from the Boston Athletic Association and race director Dave McGillivray hold the banner as Dick and Rick cross the finish in Team Hoyt's twenty-fifth Boston Marathon, April 2006. *(photorun.NET)*

Rick's first words typed on his TIC were "GO BRUINS"! In 2008, the Boston Bruins Mascot joined Rick for a picture. *(Russell Hoyt)*

Dick and Rick compete in their twenty-seventh Boston Marathon as a fellow runner cheers them on, April 2009. *(Jennifer Kohn)*

Boston Marathon Team Hoyt Charity Dinner, with Coach Uta Pippig in center of middle row, April 2009. *(Bradley Ayres Photography)*

Team Hoyt before the start of the Marlborough Massachusetts Triathlon, July 2009. *(Lynda Ruth)*

Dick and his nine siblings at their Annual Sibling Dinner, North Reading, Massachusetts, July 2009. Back row, from left: Arline, Al, Barbara, Philip, Kathy, Jason. Front Row, from left: Alice, Dick, Herbie, Ruth. *(Patricia Hoyt)*

Team Hoyt

Dad's been behind him for 65 marathons.

DEVOTION

Pass It On.

THE FOUNDATION FOR A BETTER LIFE
forbetterlife.org

Billboard of Team Hoyt representing the Foundation for a Better Life.
(Russ Dixon)

was sometimes difficult. But I had no idea it would be as hard—or as painful—as it was. Rick was loving it, and though I couldn't see the expression on his face, his hands stretched out and his fists pumped as if to say, "Faster, Dad, faster!" I went as fast as I could, but I quickly learned there was something to the idea of pacing. I tried not to worry about the runners in front of us. All but a few had disappeared from my line of vision. I just kept running. My hands quickly began to sweat against the rubber handles of Rick's chair, and I had to concentrate on both keeping my feet moving and preventing my hands from slipping and losing my grip on the chair. The other problem I hadn't anticipated was that the race was routed along a paved road with a rise along the median line, which caused us to pull to the side and, from time to time, lift one side of Rick's chair off the ground entirely. There wasn't much of a shoulder, and I worried about what lay beyond the weedy ditch. It took a lot of effort for me to run, while at the same time keep Rick's chair from swerving off the road.

I suppose we were something of a spectacle—a middle-aged man and his disabled son, wobbling down the road in a foot race. We had our supporters; I could hear our family and friends calling to us and cheering us on from the sidelines. There were the gawkers, too. People stared or pointed. I heard a lot of "Look at that!" In many ways, the looks and comments kept me going. Now I had something to prove. By the halfway point, though, I was hurting pretty bad. The cool morning air bit at my lungs and broke into a sharp heat that had me gulping for air. I had to make a conscious effort to breathe through my nose. My new sneakers had already caused blisters at the back of my heels, and my knees felt a little like Jell-O, as if they might suddenly make my body collapse into a gloppy puddle. For that reason, I was almost glad to have the wheelchair to lean on and help keep me upright. By midway, I'd long since lost track of the other runners. I knew many were well ahead. Some may have finished already. But I pressed on. For the length of the race.

When the finish line came into view, I wondered if I were dreaming. Judy, Rick's brothers, and all his friends were there, jumping and hollering and cheering us along those last few feet. Sartori's wife had her camera ready and took a picture of us as we crossed the finish line. It seemed unreal that we could have completed the race. But we had. "We did it, Rick," I gasped. Judy, the boys, and the Sartoris came running up to meet us and echoed my sentiments. "You finished!" everyone said in near disbelief. As I bent over my knees and tried to catch my breath, Rick looked up at me with that smile of his, one filled with love and thanks. I knew the aftermath of the race was going to hurt like heck, but Rick's reaction made it all worth it. I loved seeing my son so happy. "Hey, look, guys. You didn't finish last!" Rob suddenly exclaimed. "You beat that guy!" I looked to see, and sure enough, one runner crossed the finish line behind us. If I hadn't seen it with my own eyes, I'd never have believed it. Not only had we finished the race, we hadn't come in last.

As soon as we got home, Rick wanted his TIC. I wanted a nap. While Judy went to fix us a celebratory lunch and the boys scattered off to their rooms to play, I collapsed on the floor, about passed out, already hurting in muscles I didn't know I had. I remember staring up at the ceiling, feeling proud of what we had accomplished that day but realizing how old and out of shape I had become. Rick busied himself at his TIC, anxious to tell me how he felt about our performance.

When the clicking of the switch on his headrest subsided and I knew he was ready for me to read what he had written, I forced myself to get off my back and practically crawled to my son to look over his shoulder. What I read brought tears to my eyes. Rick had typed, "Dad, when I'm running, I don't feel like I'm disabled anymore." My muscles were in excruciating pain, and the irony was that while Rick was confessing that racing had made him feel free from his disability, I was feeling suddenly disabled myself. I urinated blood for three days after that run and had a hard time walking for a couple of weeks. It wasn't pretty. I felt as if my body had failed me, but reading my fifteen-year-old son's beautifully heartfelt words made it all worth it. In spite of my aching joints, I hugged Rick as tight as I could, told him I loved him, and assured him that this would not be the last race we would run together. We were a team. This was only the beginning.

In the weeks after the race, I set my sights on becoming a runner. The first order of business was getting fitted for a real pair of running shoes and starting an exercise schedule. I knew I had to begin training if I hoped to survive more than one race. Between work and the kids' school activities, I carved out time every day for running. Because our schedules didn't always mesh and sometimes Rick had schoolwork or other things to do when I was available to run, I had to be creative. I bought a hundred-pound bag of cement and ran with it in Rick's old grocery-cart wheelchair.

It wasn't just me who had to do some conditioning. Having seen what happens when you run behind a standard wheelchair for five miles and knowing that a cement bag wasn't the best stand-in for a person, I knew we had to figure a way to reconfigure Rick's chair so it was better suited for the road. The faster we found a better chair, the faster we could start entering more races. The search was on. We experimented with several ideas and even called our old friends at Tufts for advice. We went through three or four different styles of chairs, but nothing seemed quite right. One wobbled and looked rickety, another had flimsy tires.

I have to laugh when I remember some of our antics when it came to Rick's chairs. Years ago, we were on vacation and one of the wheels fell off his old shopping cart–style chair, the one we had used in the first race. We tried to buy a cart wheel from a local grocery store, but they wouldn't sell it to us. So we waited until it was dark, went back to the parking lot, and loaded up the entire cart in our van! Shopping cart wheels weren't going to cut it for racing, though, so we kept on the lookout for a better solution.

On one of our vacations in New Hampshire in 1979, when Rick was seventeen years old, I met a man who understood the problems we were having with Rick's chair and said he thought he could help us. He molded a seat that fit Rick's body, a huge improvement that alleviated our constant worry that he could slip out of his chair at any time.

Judy regularly visited Crotched Mountain Rehabilitation Center, in Greenfield, New Hampshire, to learn more about therapies for Rick. There, an engineer volunteered to build a better, runner-friendly frame for a new chair, something more aerodynamic than the shopping cart-style we'd been using. Meanwhile, I hunted for bike tires to fit the new frame. With the help of some special volunteers and a little ingenuity, for $35 the engineer finally created us a running chair based on my ideas of what might work. It looked a lot like the baby joggers of today; it had two large bicycle wheels on the sides and a smaller, third wheel at the front. It also had the specially molded seat, padded with foam to fit Rick's body and keep him in place. Now, of course, you see such contraptions everywhere, in all shapes and styles. If only we'd patented that thing, we'd be rich today!

It took three years after the Jimmy Banacos race to train and find the perfect chair for Rick. Only then did we finally feel comfortable competing and know we were ready for our first serious race. That whole time, I just kept thinking about the charity race and how it had introduced my family to an activity that my eldest son and I could share, something to strengthen our bond.

In the picture Mrs. Sartori took, you can see Rick at his most joyous. His hair is blown back, his eyes are shut, and he has the biggest grin, with his two missing front teeth. He is laughing in the wind. I'm pushing into his chair, and the right front wheel is slightly lifted off the ground, so Rick looks as if he could take off in flight. Our number, the double zero, hovers over the handlebars between my face and Rick's. Every time I look at that picture, I smile. I think how grateful I am to have Rick in my life. I think about the bond we have shared because of racing and that very first race we ran together as a team. We haven't stopped running since, and we've never finished last.

A few years ago, a man came up to me after a race and introduced himself as a high school friend of Jimmy Banacos. I asked where Jimmy was these days and how he was doing. I knew that he had moved with his family to Florida years earlier. Jimmy's friend grew quiet and said he was sorry to tell me that Jimmy passed away in 2005 after a bout with pneumonia. He had lived a long time with his paralysis, despite doctors initially giving him a five-year life expectancy. Jimmy had been awarded an honorary degree from WSC, had been married briefly, and had been working on a book at the time of his death. He kept in touch with the athletic directors at WSC and had been named to the athletes' Hall of Honor.

The Jimmy Banacos Road Race still takes place every year. The intramural department at WSC dedicated a college championship in Jimmy's honor, the James Banacos Cup. Intramural teams from a variety of sports are judged over the course of a year, and a winning team is named champion.

Everybody loved Jimmy—before and after his devastating accident. Like Rick, he had a magnetic personality and enjoyed being around people. His mother, Toulah, now widowed and in her eighties, had been the driving force behind Jimmy doing as well as he did for so long. She sought all kinds of treatment and surgeries, even some experimental ones that took them abroad. I told Jimmy's friend that day how much Jimmy had meant to me and my son, how Rick always said he needed to run that first race because he wanted to show Jimmy that life goes on despite having a disability. I wondered if Jimmy ever sensed that, if he knew how Rick felt about him and both their futures and what an impact his story had made on our lives. Though they had been our inspiration, sadly Rick and I never had a chance to meet the Banacos and thank them in person.

Chapter 10

Resistance

Three years after that first race, Rick and I were ready to compete again. We'd heard about a 10K that took place every year in nearby Springfield, Massachusetts, as part of a Greek celebration called the Glendi Festival. It sounded like fun, so we decided that the Springfield 10K would be our first official race, a way to enter the racing arena.

When we showed up the day of the race, Rick in his new running chair and me feeling much more toned and prepared for long-distance running after all my training, we met an obstacle we hadn't expected. As we made our way through the crowd, which was much larger than the one at the Jimmy Banacos charity race, there were serious runners everywhere. I got the feeling that we weren't exactly welcome. At the registration desk, the race directors looked at us with confusion. They shuffled papers, talked in whispers as if we weren't right there in front of them, and seemed reluctant to even let us register. I was surprised and a little embarrassed. This was the first time we had encountered opposition in an activity outside of school. It hardly seemed possible after how hard we had worked to get here.

It quickly became clear that many people at the Springfield 10K were opposed to our racing—from event organizers to other registered runners. The race organizers tried to explain it as a formality. For starters, there was the problem of race divisions. Races are grouped by ages, so the organizers questioned whether we should be categorized by my age or Rick's. Finally, after some talk about an issue that would follow us to subsequent races, they gave us two separate bib numbers. I would be judged in my age group and Rick would be judged in his. In the officials' eyes, it all boiled down to one problem—there was no category for us. Rick's disability would prevent him from powering his own chair, so it wouldn't be fair to the other wheelchair athletes if we competed against them. I guess they also figured that Rick and his chair would get in the way of the able-bodied runners, should we compete against them. Something as simple as signing up for a race became complicated very quickly.

It's obvious to everyone who meets me that I don't take no for an answer. I was running for Rick, who longed to be an athlete but had no way to pursue his passion. I wasn't running for my own pleasure. I was simply loaning my arms and legs to my son. I wasn't about to let the directors discourage me. After a little persuasion,

Rick and I were finally allowed to sign up for the race as official entrants, each in our own age division. But the resistance didn't stop there.

There was an overall feeling of negativity in the air. Nobody wanted Rick in a road race. Everybody, including the other participants, looked at us like we had no business being at a 10K. Nobody talked to us or wanted to have anything to do with us. A few able-bodied runners even voiced their concerns, asking why I would want to push a kid in a race when he can't even talk and just sits there in his wheelchair. I couldn't really blame them. People often were not educated about individuals with disabilities, and they'd never seen a pair like us before. It was as if Rick had some communicable disease and other runners and onlookers were wondering if they were going to catch something from him. This was a different time, a time of avoidance, which is why Rick and I do so much to encourage disability awareness now. It took a long time, but I'm happy to say that things have improved tremendously. Back then, though, we were used to the opposition.

Waiting at the starting line of the Springfield race felt different than it had waiting for the charity race to begin three years earlier. For starters, there were three hundred other runners entered in the 10K, so we were surrounded by a sea of athletes. Though I was now forty, I felt stronger and in much better condition than I had three years earlier. As we awaited the starting gun, I thought, "We can do this." Team Hoyt was ready. Then we were off. All our hard work and preparation quickly became evident. It was a much smoother ride. Rick's new running chair worked exactly as we had hoped. The bike tires gripped the road and kept us on course without veering. I felt good, too, as if I could run all day. A little over six miles was going to be nothing. I turned out to be right.

My family, though, may have underestimated Team Hoyt's athletic ability. Some family members had come to cheer us on but didn't expect us until the end of the race. They were off checking out the fair booths when we crossed the finish line.

We finished in thirty-eight minutes and thirty seconds, ahead of a hundred fifty of the three hundred runners. Judy and the boys congratulated us, and I felt pretty good about our performance. I could tell that Rick was pleased, too. His classic grin stretched from cheek to cheek. As I wiped the sweat from my brow and we discussed what we wanted to do with the rest of our day now that we had our first official race under our belts, another runner came up to shake my hand. Given the cold reception we had received, I was a little surprised. The runner, Pete Wisnewski, wanted to tell me what a great job we'd done. He was friendly and chatty, and made a great impression on me. Pete treated us as if we were any other runners who had been training and deserved to finish strong. It was a welcome improvement on what we had experienced with the other athletes and the start of our friendship. Pete, a longtime runner himself, knew all about the racing scene in Massachusetts. Later on, he and I trained together. Because he was a faster runner than Rick and me, he really inspired me to improve my stamina and speed.

After the Glendi 10K, weekends in 1980 were reserved for racing. Nearly every weekend we found a race somewhere. Rick and I loved getting up early on a Saturday; I would load the running chair into our van, and away we'd go. Sometimes we ventured outside Massachusetts. Often, our new friend Pete Wisnewski would go along. Pete introduced us to the idea of running longer distances.

Sometimes, Rick and I would run as many as three races, one during the week and then back to back on both Saturday and

Sunday. It was like we couldn't quit. Rick was the driving force behind all that running. Race after race, he would get home and ask on his computer, "When's the next one?" I worried about him a little because he had such a competitive spirit. Sometimes midrace, if he saw another runner ahead of us he thought we could beat, he would get so excited and thrash around in his chair that I'd have to tell him to take it easy or he'd tip over. The father-son coaching went both ways. Rick made me push myself, but not too hard. He would listen to my breathing during a race. If it got too labored, he would turn his head around and let me know it with a look that said, "Your turn to take it easy, Dad." We made a great team, and as we went from race to race, people finally started to accept the idea of us competing together. But it was an uphill battle.

When we first started making a name for ourselves and officially competing, reporters began to tell our story in newspapers and magazines. I got letters from people with disabled family members who were pretty upset and wanted to know why I was dragging my son through all those races. What they didn't realize was that my son was the one dragging *me* through all those different races. Rick was the one who wanted to run. I thought that if that was all he requested of me—that I run a few miles and push him in a wheelchair—then that was the least I could do for my child.

Around 1980, we started evaluating our three-race weeks. The more we raced, the stronger we got. In a week of three races, we always seemed to run the third race the fastest, as if we were just catching our stride. That's when it occurred to me that, like our friend Pete, we could surely run much longer distances than the 5Ks or 10Ks we had been racing. Pete agreed and told us we should go for it. That's when we decided we would run the grand-daddy of all marathons: the Boston Marathon.

In late winter of 1980, I mailed our entry application for the Boston Marathon to the Boston Athletic Association (BAA). Two weeks later, we got a response. Our application had been rejected. We would not be allowed to run the race as official entrants, and we didn't qualify for the wheelchair division. Given the trouble we had had registering for the 10K in Springfield, I wasn't too surprised. I figured I would simply have to keep after the BAA until the organizers relented. I called and wrote probably a dozen times between that first application and April, when the race took place. The answer was always the same—you can't run the marathon because you don't qualify for any of the divisions. Finally, I think they caved a little, just so I would quit pestering them. Race officials compromised by saying we could run the race, but we wouldn't be given a number, and we would have to line up behind the wheelchair entrants. So, we could run, but only as unofficial entrants. Or, as runners deem anyone who takes part in a race without paying the entry fee, we could run as bandits.

I wasn't thrilled about the idea of being seen as an outlaw, but as the marathon approached, it seemed our only option. We couldn't *not* run the Boston Marathon. There was something in both Rick and me that compelled us to run that race. It was our hometown race. We felt we belonged there and were ready to give it a try.

In the months leading up to the marathon, I'd amped up my training and had been running greater distances for longer times. While Rick was at school and unable to train with me, I turned back to my trusty cement bag for practice. Despite all the work we had put in, I knew that if we had any hope of finishing a marathon, and doing well, we needed to run a race longer than ten miles.

As usual, our running buddy Pete came up with the solution. He knew about an eighteen-mile race called the Chop-a-Thon in Albany, New York, which took place one month before the Boston Marathon. It seemed like the perfect practice race. If we could run eighteen miles, I told Rick, we could just as easily run twenty-six. What were a few extra miles, I reasoned. We set our sights on New York.

The day of the Albany race was miserable. Upstate New York in March was exactly what you might expect—snowy and frigid. We were Massachusetts men though. I knew we could handle it. And if we couldn't, I knew we had no business running a marathon in Boston. The morning of the race, we bundled Rick up with several layers of sweat suits, a cap, gloves, and sunglasses. We probably added twenty pounds to the kid. He wasn't going to be cold, that was for sure.

A Channel 4 Boston reporter, Barry Nolan, had followed us to Albany based on a tip from a woman who was vying to win a contest to help the station find the "Most Inspirational Boston Marathon Story." The Team Hoyt story eventually won the contest, before we attempted the Boston Marathon, and the woman who entered it won a trip to Hawaii! Before the Albany race began, I told Nolan that our goal was to run a seven-minute pace. I remember how surprised and doubtful he looked. But we had been training hard. In snow or sunshine, I felt we could do it.

Team Hoyt had something to prove before we could attempt the marathon. It was a cold, cold eighteen miles, but I felt good to be out there running for that stretch of time, pushing Rick. Judy, Rob, and Russ followed in the van on a road that ran alongside the race route. They'd roll down the windows or stop every so often and get out to cheer us on. I'd wave when I saw them, and it pushed me to go even harder. There were thirteen hundred other runners in the Albany Chop-a-Thon, and with a finish time of two hours and six minutes, we beat nine hundred of them. Nolan was there at the finish line to tell us we'd met our goal of a seven-minute pace. When he asked what was next, I answered right away: Boston.

Our strong finish in the Chop-a-Thon went a long way toward establishing our credibility, but I sensed that we still were going to face some resistance when we came to Boston. We were, after all, running as bandits—a disappointing category to be in—but there seemed to be no way around it. We still had to prove ourselves. It's hard to look back and remember that once, in the racing world, people weren't so accepting of me or my son. After all the races we had run and the time we'd put in, attitudes slowly began to shift. I credit Rick and his ability to win people over. All it took was someone to approach us, talk to Rick, and see him as a person. Runners and racing fans were beginning to recognize that we were serious about competing and that it meant everything to Rick to be able to participate in a sport that had been almost exclusively for the able-bodied or those who were disabled but had some control over their own physicality. For the sake of my son, I cast aside any thoughts about resistance or obstacles and looked forward to Boston.

On the big day of the marathon, April 20, 1981, we arrived at the starting point in the town of Hopkinton four hours early. I had never been so anxious about a race before. I knew this was big, for both Rick and me. We were hoping to finish in three hours. I kept checking Rick's chair and probably drove him crazy by asking how he felt and making sure he was doing alright. I tried to keep as low a profile as possible. Truthfully, I was terrified that officials would yank us from the race at the last minute. Finally, they announced that the race was about to start and that wheelchair athletes should be ready to go. We fell in line, and I told Rick to hold on. Official runners or not, we were off in the Boston Marathon. It was amazing being among all those athletes and hearing the roar of the onlookers, a crowd like I'd never witnessed before. I felt exhilarated—for about the first twenty miles.

Then, around mile twenty-two, it hit me. Or I hit it—the wall. My legs were on fire, my lungs ached, and even my arms hurt. At times, I felt I might vomit all the water I chugged before the race began. It was bitter cold, so when the wind hit my chest, I thought my upper body might be freezing. It hurt so bad that I was forced to walk for a while. I knew I'd blown our three-hour goal. Surprisingly, though, the other runners were supportive. They'd reach out and pat my back, call out "Way to go" as they ran past, and encouraged me to hang in there. And though those pats on my back felt as if they weighed five hundred pounds, they were inspiring. The Red Sox game traditionally played on the day of the race had ended before we reached the final stretch near Fenway Park, but fans had stuck around to cheer the marathoners. They were cheering for us. Rick nearly flipped his chair, he got so excited at the applause.

We crossed the finish line in Copley Square (in front of the Prudential Tower), our first marathon ever, after three hours and eighteen minutes of racing—a seven-and-a-half-minute pace. Rick and I were cold, exhausted, and disappointed to have not quite met our goal. But we had finished. We had run the Boston Marathon.

Not long after the marathon was over, Nolan aired a follow-up story on us on Channel 4 Boston. That broadcast really put us on the map, and I was reinvigorated by the praise we received.

I talked about Rick, his chair, and his TIC, so Tufts Medical Center received some recognition, which turned into funding for other projects. Rick and I both felt like overnight celebrities. We didn't know quite what to do with the newfound attention. I only hoped the ruckus would work to make it easier for us to get into future races—the Boston Marathon included. We quickly resumed training and planning another year of racing. All the while, I kept thinking about Boston. About next year. About running faster and better and as official race entrants instead of bandits.

In the piece Nolan did, he asked if we would ever run the Boston Marathon again. I told him we would run it next year, but we would do it in three hours. It was a promise I aimed to keep.

Chapter 11

The Boston Marathon

S ince our first time running as bandits, Rick and I have run the Boston Marathon twenty-seven times. It's the one race we have almost never missed since we started running competitively. That's how important the race is to us. We have only had to miss twice, once in 2003 because I had just had a heart attack, and once in 2007, when Rick was recovering from surgery. That is pretty revealing about our allegiance to the event.

Something about the Boston Marathon keeps us coming back year after year. It's not just that it is one of the world's oldest marathons. It's not necessarily the mystique that surrounds the race, either, its Greek origins, or the huge crowds that turn out every year. Nor is it the hoopla that surrounds Patriots' Day, a holiday commemorating the anniversary of the first battles of the American Revolution. Or the big game at Fenway Park where the Red Sox have played at home every year since 1959. All of that is enticing and makes for an exciting marathon. But what truly makes Boston special is that, in the simplest terms—it's our hometown race.

The Boston Marathon is the first one we ever completed, so naturally it holds a special place in our hearts. Just a drive away from where our children were raised, in my eyes, it's the perfect race. The event has allowed my son and me to join one of the highest profile races in the world, as well as feel like legitimate athletes, even though it took officials a while to recognize that.

In an article written about us a few years ago for *Runner's World*, Jack Fleming, a spokesman for the BAA, reflected on how Rick and I have become recognized participants in the marathon. "They personify the race as much as the elite athletes do," Fleming is quoted as saying. He goes on: "They are also quintessential New England guys. The crowds love them." Words like that make us feel welcome, as if we really belong, which is especially fulfilling after the hard work it took for us to get people to reach that perspective.

One of the main reasons we run every year in Boston is that it's gratifying to know we not only fit in somewhere but we also are respected. People want to meet us and share their own stories, something I find incredibly touching every time it happens. Total strangers come up to us before the race and shake our hands, pat us on the back, and say, "We look forward to seeing you every year. It's not a Boston Marathon unless we see you two running." They want to take our picture and wish us good luck.

The best part of the Boston race is the expo in the days leading up to the marathon. There are booths with free samples and marathon paraphernalia. You get to meet people from all over the globe. That's our favorite part, which is probably why we began setting up our own Team Hoyt booth every year. We love meeting all those people, many of whom want to talk to me and Rick and share their own challenges and successes. Other fathers and sons, mothers and daughters, husbands and wives talk to us about how their bonds were strengthened because of running. It's the same with Rick and me, so seeing that reflected in others makes us feel as if we are making a difference in other people's lives.

Despite the hundreds of other races we have run and miles we have logged, the Boston Marathon is our favorite race and the one we look forward to every year. It has allowed me to develop a very special relationship with my son, forged because we discovered our love of running together. Rick and I both say that, if we can only do one race a year, it will be Boston. We were destined to be runners in it. But it took a while to get others to realize that.

After our first Boston Marathon in 1981, I set out to make good on my promise that the following year, we wouldn't enter the race as bandits, but as official runners. Like most things in my world, that was easier said than done. Between our first Boston Marathon and the following one, Rick and I had been busy running, finishing more than fifty other races. I probably wrote as many letters to the BAA, trying to convince the officials to let us run as official entrants. Every time I wrote or called with proof that Rick and I were capable and deserved a position amid the official runners—no matter if my proof was telling them about our strong finish in another long race or how we had never had an injury—the answer was always no. I even got in touch with Will Cloney, then the race's executive director. He was sympathetic but remained firm, saying there was simply nothing he could do to bend the rules and allow us to officially participate. I understood where he was coming from, but in my family, we'd learned long ago that sometimes rules need adjusting. At the very least, we deserved a shot. Despite the disappointment, Rick and I kept up our routine as usual, sensing that all our training would eventually pay off.

Unfortunately, it did not pay off in 1982, when we once again were forced to run our hometown race as bandits. I did make good on one promise, however. We ran it in just under three hours, clocking in at two hours and fifty-nine minutes. And the media took notice. Even BAA officials congratulated us on our achievement. Reporters were so impressed, they started asking me if I ever considered running on my own—without my son. It was the first time anyone had ever suggested it, and I was pretty shocked. I guess it had never occurred to me. Although I was happy that people were beginning to view me, especially at my age, as a competitive athlete, I was quick to respond that I would never run without my son. He was the reason I had taken up running in the first place. We continued to do so for the sake of all the other disabled people who didn't have the opportunities that we did. We always wanted to raise awareness, and while I'm able to do that, I will. Besides, without Rick, I wouldn't have known what to do with my arms.

Before we realized it, another year had passed. Though hard to believe, Rick was a senior at Westfield High School when the 1983 Boston Marathon rolled around. Judy had finished a graduate degree in special education. Rob was living on his own and working a good job, and Russ was a high school wrestling star. Rick and I were running seemingly nonstop. We had gained notoriety and public support, but I still had to convince the BAA that we were ready to compete officially in Boston. When first pressed, the answer was still the same—Rick and I could run unofficially, but since Rick was not running and unable to push his own chair himself, I was considered the only athlete on our team. It was frustrating, to say the least. We felt welcome, in that we were at least allowed to run the race, but we were tired of being bandits. At least, I was. I didn't like being a part of something that at the same time made me feel excluded. Rick used to say it didn't matter to him one way or the other, as long as his friends and family were there to cheer him on. That's what he looked forward to every year.

I was continually glad for Rick's positive attitude, but official recognition was important to me. It was one more hurdle we had to jump over to get others to realize that persons with disabilities are no less able or worthy than those without disabilities. In my eyes, Rick was an athlete—he could be anything he wanted to be and do anything he wanted to do. Sometimes, we had to get creative for that to happen, but I had every confidence in my son.

Finally, with the media on our side, the BAA compromised. It was too late to make any difference for the 1983 marathon. However, the BAA said that in the future we could run the race officially—if we met the specified requirements. The news was promising, but it wasn't without a catch. What it meant was that we had to run fast enough to qualify. And we had to run fast enough, not in my age division (three hours and ten minutes), but in Rick's age division. In order to qualify as official runners, we had to run another officially sanctioned marathon in two hours and fifty minutes, the requirement for any twenty-year-old runner. How much you want to bet those directors thought we would never do it? How much you want to bet I was determined to prove them wrong? That year, we bested our prior record and ran the Boston Marathon in two hours and fifty-eight minutes. It wasn't good enough to officially qualify us, but it was close. We set out to make it even closer.

Rick and I started running every race we could, and then race directors started inviting us. Our story had spread, and we began receiving almost more invitations to run in races than we could actually accept. We did as many as we could—long or short, charity or sponsored—considering it all practice for Boston. Remember that Rick was in school, and I was still working full-time. It was a balancing act, but one Rick and I felt was worthwhile. I wanted to qualify more than anything. Finally, our buddy Pete Wisnewski suggested the Marine Corps Marathon in Washington, D.C. It's a big race that draws a lot of runners and has a great course. Since it took place in the fall instead of the dead of winter, it seemed our chances were better at hitting the qualifying time of two hours and fifty minutes. I sensed that this was the one.

October of 1983, the weekend before Halloween, it was cool and rainy in D.C. It wasn't nearly as cold as it had been in Boston earlier that year, though, so for that we were grateful. And optimistic. Rick, as ever, was a good sport and took my seriousness with a grain of salt. The morning of the Marine Corps Marathon, when I went into Rick's room to get him ready for the day, he was waiting with a shaved head (thanks to his brothers), a Marine uniform that he'd managed to purchase, and a salute. Rick has always known how to take some of the pressure off, and he can always sense when I am nervous before a race and need to calm down.

After a good laugh at seeing him in his Marine getup, I dressed him more appropriately for the marathon, triple-checked all the elements on his running chair, and we set off for a marathon around the nation's capital. Just imagine what it's like to run amid patriotic fervor, surrounded by historic monuments at every turn. The crowd was huge—the marathon is the fifth largest in the United States, tenth largest in the world. Because it's the largest of its kind not to offer prize money for the winner, most folks have taken to calling it "The People's Marathon." There were certainly plenty of people there to witness the race. Among the able-bodied athletes were quite a few wheelchair participants, and we lined up alongside them. At the starting gun, I took off, and we blazed through the first ten miles in just over an hour—plenty fast enough to make our goal. I tried to pace myself from there on out. As we neared the finish line, I couldn't get a good look at the time clock. But I saw Rick reacting, pumping his arms in the air. When we crossed the finish line to applause like I'd never heard before, I knew we'd done it.

Our official time for The People's Marathon was 2:45:30. Doug Donaldson, a journalist who wrote a piece on us for the magazine *Heart-Healthy Living* in summer 2007, explained the accomplishment: "Think of it this way: The duo has finished faster than Lance Armstrong in the 2006 New York City Marathon. And most hard-core runners train for years and aspire to such a sub-3-hour time." Now I'm generally not one to go on about my own abilities, but after that Marine Corps Marathon, I knew we had done something big. So many people came up and congratulated us afterward, it was overwhelming. Even Bill Rodgers, one of my personal heroes who had won the Boston Marathon four times, told a reporter for *People Weekly* magazine that Rick and I were world-class athletes: "Everyone involved in the sport of marathoning is inspired by the Hoyts." I can't quite express how humbling it was to be spoken of so highly by an athlete I thoroughly respected.

Mostly, though, I was relieved that Rick and I had done it. I knew that because we were nearly five minutes under the mandated qualifying time, we would finally be cleared to run as official entrants in the Boston Marathon. As soon as we got home from D.C., I filled out our application. I even got Rick to sign with an X. Soon after, the BAA granted us permission to run the race—officially. It was an exciting day, another huge hurdle overcome by Team Hoyt.

Given our triumph with the Boston Marathon, more and more people wanted to tell our story, and 1984 proved to be a big year for us Hoyts. *Hour Magazine*, a nationally syndicated television show, did a piece on us right before the 1984 marathon. It seemed as if anyone who lived in Boston recognized us from the show. Without a doubt, everyone running the race that day knew our names. The BAA officials had obviously seen the television special as well, and given our history with them, they knew our names. In the expo days leading up to the marathon, as we prepped for the race and went through the usual registration tasks—before we were given our first legitimate Boston Marathon entry number—BAA committee members asked my son and me to talk to the media and help publicize the event. I recognized the irony in their request, but I was glad to help.

As long as we weren't bandits any longer, I was happy. Rick loved the extra attention. He said that he felt like a celebrity. That was a marathon to remember. Just knowing that we were official entrants made an amazing difference. Getting to run alongside all those other elite, qualified athletes was quite an experience. Our newfound celebrity didn't hinder our performance. We finished the 1984 Boston Marathon in two hours and fifty minutes, five seconds, good enough to beat our best Boston time ever.

Not only were we included, we were also successful. There is no better feeling in the world.

That first year we ran as official entrants, we accomplished another goal—Rick graduated from high school. We started making plans for the next step, which was college and independence. My little boy had become a young man. I could not have been more impressed with the ways in which he had grown and matured. My first-born son had turned into a young adult. He had also become my best friend. It was clear to everyone who knew us how far our family had come. It was a special time in our lives, being able to reflect on all that we had accomplished since Rick was born.

We also reflected on the past several years and the journey we had gone on with our hometown race. Not only had our relationship grown, but we had developed a new relationship with running. The Boston Marathon had played a huge role in making that possible. We were official marathoners. The title would follow us for many years. In fact, for the marathon's one-hundredth anniversary in 1996, the race's organizer and sponsor recognized Rick and me as honorary Centennial Heroes. It was incredible to be a part of such a celebration and recognized by a race in which we had invested so much.

But in 1984, that recognition was years away. We had more races to run, more Boston Marathons to complete. If we accomplished that feat, I knew there were even greater adventures in racing ahead of us yet to discover.

Chapter 12

Triathlons

I n the midst of getting Rick settled in college—after much debate, he had decided on Boston University, a fitting choice, given our victories in Boston—I decided to become a triathlete. The challenge had come at another race, just before the Marine Corps Marathon where we made our Boston qualifying time. It had come from a fellow runner.

The Falmouth 7.1-mile race was one of our favorite races and we tried to run it every year. It was a short little jaunt compared to the marathons we'd been training for, but still fun and good practice. Since it was practically in the backyard of where we had once lived, and because Judy's parents still had a place in nearby Cape Cod, it always felt like going back home—a family reunion of sorts. We considered Falmouth another hometown race, like the Boston Marathon. We were always welcomed with open arms.

In August 1983, after the Falmouth race, fans began to gather around us. "I've heard of you two before," one athlete said. "You're Dick and Rick Hoyt. It's nice to meet you guys." That athlete was Dave McGillivray, who ran a sports enterprise in the Boston area. He became a lifelong friend. He was also a triathlete and a pioneer for the sport throughout the Northeast. He was complimentary of our performance and said, "Dick, you look like you'd make a great triathlete. You gotta try triathlons." I kind of laughed when he suggested it—didn't triathlons mean swimming? I asked—but realized he was sincere. I told him that sure, I'd do a triathlon, but only if Rick could do one with me. Well, that ended the offer. Dave took one look at Rick in his chair and turned and walked away.

A whole year went by, and we were back at the same race in Falmouth when Dave came back up to me and said, "C'mon Dick. You're in better shape now. You've mastered the marathon. You have to do triathlons." Without hesitating, I gave him the same answer as I had the year before. Somewhat to my surprise, he said that he wanted Team Hoyt to run an endurance triathlon called the Bay State Triathlon that he sponsored in Medford, Massachusetts. He suggested I see what types of equipment I could get built so that Rick and I could compete together, and he would make it happen. I was floored and excited by the possibility of competing in a triathlon with my son.

Ever since we'd met Dave the previous year, Rick had been after me because this was something he wanted to do. He was really pumped up about it. Never mind the inherent difficulties involved in figuring out how to get Rick on a bike and in the water. I hadn't been on a bike since I was six years old. I didn't know how to swim. It would be an undertaking like none I had ever attempted, but Rick was insistent. On the spot, at our annual Falmouth race, I committed to running Dave's triathlon. If he could get us in, I could handle the rest. If it hadn't been for Dave, we probably would never have done triathlons.

I told Dave I would see what I could do about properly equipping Team Hoyt for a race that wasn't just running but swimming and biking, too. We had about nine months to prepare. To complicate matters, I was in the process of changing jobs. The Air National Guard had promoted me and wanted me to transfer to Wellesley, right outside Boston. Judy was happy in Westfield, Russ was still in high school, and here I was looking to get us into a whole new sport. With the promotion and everything else going on, I got to thinking that if I were going to do triathlons and do them right, I was going to have to learn how to swim. In my mind, that meant I should buy a house on a lake, which is exactly what I did. Judy and I had always dreamed of owning a lakefront home. Since I was looking at the possibility of retirement in the next few years, I convinced the family it was a good idea. We found a great cottage in Holland, Massachusetts, surrounded by long, hilly, country roads (perfect for our bike training) and right on a pretty little lake called Hamilton Reservoir (just like a pool in my backyard). The house needed a lot of work, but that appealed to me, since I'd been doing masonry work for years. It was time I had the chance to do some work on my own place again. With the purchase of a house on a lake, that's how it all started.

Participating in a triathlon is not the same as running a marathon. My kids quickly reminded me when I told them my big plans for buying a house on the water that I didn't know how to swim. Swimming was going to be a challenge on its own. Rob, who had swum competitively throughout high school, could attest that it was hard work and was a lot different than running. I learned that real quick.

After we'd moved in, I decided to give the lake a try. I went to the water, jumped in, and promptly sank to the bottom. It was a rude awakening. I tried every stroke, arm movement, and leg-kicking combination I could come up with, but I just couldn't get all my limbs to cooperate. I couldn't breathe and didn't understand how to hold my breath and come up for air while moving through the water. It was so different from putting one foot in front of the other and powering through the hurt of a run. I knew this was really going to be a challenge.

Rob did his best to explain breathing methods and even got in the water and showed me how to float and move my arms at the same time. But it just took me sticking to it, like anything else I guess. All summer long, I jumped in that water every day. Each time, I'd make it out a little farther and could hold my breath a little longer. When the reservoir water got too cold, I bought my first wetsuit. When winter in Massachusetts really set in, I joined the local YMCA and swam laps in the indoor pool.

I started feeling more comfortable in the water, but there was still the question of how we were going to get Rick in alongside me. I knew I'd have to pull him in some kind of conveyance, and the only thing I could come up with was a boat. One day I saw one of my neighbors paddling an inflatable raft across the reservoir and knew that was my answer. It would be lighter than any boat or canoe, and its high sides would still keep Rick safe and dry. After word got out that I was in the market for an inflatable raft to tow my son in triathlons, a friend at the Falmouth Yacht Club offered to donate a brand-new, nine-foot inflatable dinghy, then made by Boston Whaler. It was perfect. I figured I could easily string a line between my body and the raft, and considered my options for finding sturdy enough materials to do so. As I'd done so many times before when looking for camping gear, I hit up the supply officer at the base. The solution? Old parachute strappings that I rigged with a tether. The only thing left was to make sure Rick had a comfortable ride. We considered putting a wood floor in the bottom of the dinghy, but that defeated the purpose of making the raft light and maneuverable. Ultimately, we wound up deciding on a beanbag, handmade by Judy's sister Nancy, in California.

The swimming portion taken care of, I moved on to figuring out the bike. Riding a bicycle turned out to have a much easier learning curve than swimming had. Again, though, we had to figure a way that I could safely tow or push Rick from my perch on a bike. I found a guy in Longmeadow, Massachusetts, who built racing bikes and frames. I told him about a chair design I'd been thinking about. I had an idea that I could pull Rick behind me, trailer style, in a chair that, with a simple switch of the wheels, could then easily convert for the running portion. This would eliminate moving Rick from one chair to another and save time. The racing bike builder liked my idea and said he could fabricate it, but it wouldn't be cheap. A new eighteen-speed Trek bike and running chair was going to cost over $4,000. And we had to arrange for orthopedic doctors in Springfield to help us mold the perfect seat to fit Rick and keep him secure throughout the ride. Rick and I had to do some finagling to convince his mother it was a good investment. But since we had already registered for the triathlon, she eventually caved in and let us have our way.

The final equipment preparations for our first triathlon were not complete until one week before the race. That meant our first practice run out on the lake, with Rick in the inflatable raft, took place a few short days before the real deal. It was early summer, and the lake was busy with boaters and skiers; the waves they were creating made me pretty nervous. My goal was to make a lap around the lake, which I'd guessed was about a mile—the distance we would be swimming for the triathlon. Judy and one of my brothers, Phillip, were there to help get Rick situated in the dinghy. Then they followed in a motor boat so they could watch us and steer other boats clear.

We got in the water and I knew right away it was going to be a lot different from my early morning swim alone. For one, in addition to being windy, there was a strong current. Those waves the other boats were making put up quite a resistance. I splashed around and kicked about as best I could, but it was tough maintaining a straight path. It took us an hour, and throughout the entire swim, I could hear Rick in the boat, laughing. From time to time, I'd look back to be sure the beanbag was keeping him propped up and that water wasn't filling the boat. There was Rick—lying back, happy as a clam.

Rick has never had any fear. If he could jump out of a plane, he would do it. He has always gravitated toward new experiences. He was then only in his early twenties—the prime of young adulthood. Like any guy that age, he was looking for adventure. I was always the one more afraid for Rick and how he would handle racing. The practice swim proved a success, so we felt pretty good about the swimming portion of the quickly approaching triathlon. We still weren't able to try out Rick's new bike. The custom seat we had ordered hadn't arrived. It was delivered on Saturday, one day before the triathlon, so there was no time for a test run.

If I had any preconceived notions about what participating in a triathlon was going to be like, those were quickly thrown out the window as we took our starting place at Spot Pond for the Bay State Triathlon in Medford on Father's Day, 1985. It was quite a Father's Day celebration, racing a triathlon for the first time. Most people, in their first attempt, do a sprint triathlon, which consists of a swim of maybe a third of a mile, a nine- to twelve-mile bike ride, and maybe a 5K run. Dave's Bay State Triathlon consisted of a one-mile swim, a forty-mile bike ride, and a ten-mile run. We knew the ten miles weren't going to be a problem. It was getting through the swim and the bike segments beforehand that had me nervous. We weren't the average triathlete who arrives with a bike and Speedo and is ready to go. We had a lot of prep work before each leg of the race. We had to inflate the boat and get that ready, set up my bike and put Rick's chair on it, and then do the wheel conversion to the running chair.

I realized this first triathlon was going to be a trial run. But as I pulled on my wetsuit and we got Rick situated in the dinghy, I started to feel excited—a feeling different than even running our first marathon. I got the sense that, though we still got our fair share of stares and even a "What the heck?" or two, it was clear most people knew who we were. We were the infamous Team Hoyt who had conquered the Boston Marathon. Dave announced to the crowd as the other athletes gathered that

Rick and I were competing in our first triathlon, and he hoped the other participants would give us a hand if we needed it. What a confidence boost! When the other athletes saw us unloading and setting up all our equipment, they knew we were serious about competing. People started to consider us members of their club. I felt like a real athlete.

On that very hot day, as I waded into the cool water of Spot Pond with Rick in tow, I wondered how I had gotten myself into this. It was crazy that I was about to swim a mile, towing a dinghy with my full-grown son in it, having just learned to swim in the past year. But all I had to do was look back at Rick and know how excited he was. I knew I had to try my best. The starting gun fired, and we were off. At first, the water churned with the strokes of all the swimmers. We were right there in the pack. I tried to keep to the outside edge to prevent the others from colliding into Rick's boat. Everyone was mindful, so that turned out not to be an issue at all. After the initial flurry, the waters calmed and I set our pace.

It was much easier than swimming in the reservoir on a busy summer boating day. In less than an hour, we had completed the swim, faster than our practice time and certainly faster than I had expected us to do. As I got out of my wetsuit and Rick out of his inflatable boat and life preserver, Rick was all smiles. It was a two-hundred yard dash across the sand, my grown son in my arms, to our untested running bike. I was most nervous about this part, but honestly, I knew that if I had managed to complete a one-mile swim without dog paddling or overturning the boat I was towing, the rest would be a piece of cake. My chief concern was the new bike and running chair combo we hadn't yet had a chance to test.

The course turned out to be very hilly. The wind picked up. The conditions for a forty-mile bike ride in the sweltering June heat were not the best. I could feel the chair I towed whipping back and forth, but since it was six feet behind me, I had a hard time keeping an eye on Rick and making sure he wasn't about to roll over. When I did manage to look back, I could see how excited he was. I had to imagine how exhilarated he must feel, going fast with the wind in his face. We had never achieved such speed by running, so I could tell he loved it. Still, with the somewhat precarious and untested new bike racing chair, I wanted to err on the side of caution. I kept my pace in check and trusted that the happy noises Rick was making meant that everything was okay. Other bikers would blaze past and cheer us on, giving me a thumbs-up as they went around us. I was relieved, however, to get to the running part of the race. I disconnected the chair from my bike and attached the wheel back to the front, tied on my running shoes, and we were off. This was our specialty. Ten miles was nothing, and we did it in one hour and five minutes.

The triathlon took us over four hours, but we finished. Just as in our very first race, we came in next to last, but not last. I thought this was a fine showing, considering the odds against us. Dave was there at the finish to ask how we thought it went. I joked that we could have been faster, had Rick not taken a little nap. In truth, we felt great. The crowd and the other racers were so supportive. Scott Tinley, who won the triathlon that year and set a new course record, congratulated us. I found out later that we'd shaken hands with a celebrity. Tinley was a former winner of Ironman Hawaii.

I was invited to the microphone to say a few words during the awards ceremony. It was the first time I had been given the chance to publicly credit the real winner of all Team Hoyt's races: my son Rick. If it hadn't been for him, I said, I probably would weigh three hundred pounds and be lounging around in a bar somewhere. It was the truth. I knew it then, and I know it now. The other truth was that we had loved our first triathlon. We were hooked. Triathlon freaks, I called us, as my son looked on happily. We couldn't wait to enter again.

Chapter 13

Ironmen

After that first triathlon and Rick and I became triathlon freaks, we entered every one that we could fit into our schedule. In 1986, we even challenged Rick's youngest brother, Russ, to compete against us. Not surprisingly, we beat him, but only by a few minutes. Russ was definitely a stronger swimmer than me, but all of us knew there would be no contest when it came to the running portion. Rick and I had honed our racing to a fine craft, and we had clocked marathon times that were mere minutes from world records. Russ was, quite literally, a fish out of water, and we were seasoned runners who were none too bad on a bike, either.

By then, Rick and I were triathlon veterans and our calendar was full, another year packed with weekend races. That's when I got a phone call in early spring. At the other end was Lyn von Ert, the race director of Ironman Canada. She wanted to up the ante. She had called to invite us to participate in the event at the end of August.

I knew more than a little something about the Ironman organization. Anyone who competes in triathlons keeps a hopeful eye on Ironman. It is the cream of the crop, as far as competitions go. It's also an event designed to showcase the most serious triathletes. Ironman Canada would involve racing on unfamiliar terrain for longer distances than any triathlon we had yet competed in. Though Rick and I had talked about doing bigger triathlons, I didn't know that we were prepared to become Ironmen. I hadn't been sure what to make of Lyn's offer. "Are you pulling my leg?" I had asked. She told me they would be willing to pay all our expenses if we wanted to compete. She was serious. It sounded like an opportunity we couldn't pass up.

Initially, Rick thought I was out of my mind to accept. Maybe I was. I knew the 2.4-mile swim would be tough, and 112 miles on a bike followed by a marathon-length run was almost unfathomable. But we had a new tandem racing bike, thanks to the engineering company XRE. We had gotten our swims down to a science. Rick thought about it. I thought about it. You can guess our conclusion. Before we knew it, it was August 31, and we were in Penticton, British Columbia, on the shores of Lake Okanagan.

Though we didn't complete that first Ironman race before the seventeen-hour cutoff time, we did finish, and once again, we didn't finish last. We crossed the line to some pretty incredible fanfare. "Chariots of Fire" was blasting from the speakers. Champagne was being poured, and throngs of supporters were there to make sure we would make it, which we did at nearly one a.m. The race had been no cakewalk. My legs nearly gave out, and Rick had suffered a little dehydration.

Only after, I found out that Ironman Canada has a reputation as one of the hardest races in the world, because the course is so challenging. I'm one of those guys who would rather take a race in stride and deal with challenges as they present themselves during an event, so I rarely check out the course before a race. At Penticton, however, some reporters from *Parade* magazine who were doing a feature story on us and chronicling our first Ironman had gone out the day before the race to look at the course. When they came back, they announced, "There's no way you can finish the bike race." This was seven hours before Rick and I were to start competing. I didn't pay any attention to the reporters who thought the course would be too difficult for us. We've faced that kind of skepticism before.

Ironman Canada certainly wasn't easy. The mountain part of the race route, Richter Pass, had the steepest inclines we had ever biked. It was grueling, but we recovered. Rick did the whole thing with his usual sense of humor, sporting a Mohawk he'd had fashioned right before the race. I joked that the extra hair sticking up on top of his head sure didn't have a streamlining effect.

A couple weeks later, *People* magazine ran a story about Rick and me in Canada. The response was incredible. It became clear that we had a quickly growing fan base, people who not only recognized us but sent us letters of admiration, just because they'd seen us competing. Folks all over the racing community were taking notice.

"What's next, Rick? Think we can beat this?" I asked my son after we had returned home to the states. The *People* article had just come out, and we were already seeing the outpouring of support, the encouragement to keep at it. True to form, Rick smiled and laughed, pleased with the positive attention and ready for the next adventure.

Ironman Canada had been a real challenge, possibly the most difficult we had ever attempted. Not surprisingly, it only made us hungry for more. I set my sights on the big Kahuna: Ironman Hawaii. It is the world's championship, where the best triathletes from all over gather to compete. It is the ultimate test of body and heart. While there are thousands of triathlons around the world, this is the one that athletes associate with being the best of the sport. It is triathlon's version of the Super Bowl, Wimbledon, the World Series, the Tour de France . . . you get the idea. According to the informational brochures, thousands of triathletes apply to snag one of the coveted Ironman World spots every year. Only 1,800 make it to the starting point in Kona, Hawaii.

The original Ironman is the most punishing endurance racing. Hawaiian waters are warm, so wetsuits are not allowed. There's no added help from their buoyancy. The cycling hills are steep and often undercut with gusting winds. The marathon portion along the coast of the Big Island, with the crosswinds from lava fields at your back, makes for a steamy run.

I felt a special connection to the Ironman because the event had started around the time when Rick and I first began racing. In 1977, it began as a challenge at an awards ceremony for a relay running race in Honolulu. A group of local athletes had discussed the idea of starting an annual endurance triathlon by combining three major events already held on the island—ocean swimming, lava desert biking, and a marathon along the island's coast. U.S. Navy Commander John Collins had suggested combining them and creating a single-day event. At the relay race awards ceremony, Commander Collins announced the event and promised, "Whoever finishes first, we'll call the Ironman." What Commander Collins said about the event is what is especially meaningful to me— Ironman is about finishing what you started. You might not finish first or as fast as the person who finishes in front of you, but at least you finish. It's a message that is perfectly aligned with Team Hoyt's thinking. We had to compete in that race.

As with any triathlon on that scale, you have to qualify in order to compete. To do that, you must win your age division in another qualifying race in the Ironman Series, win the Ironman Lottery, or—a rarer occurrence—receive a special invitation. Rick and I were determined to try, so during the application process we continued to run Ironman-length events like the Hyannis Endurance Triathlon. In Hyannis, we had a good swim portion, often the most difficult leg for us of any triathlon. We made it back in an hour and fifty minutes, half an hour faster than we had done in Canada. We biked the flat course in under eight hours, two hours faster than we had biked through Richter Pass. Our goal for Hyannis, which we thought would get us noticed by Ironman Hawaii, was twelve hours. We finished in 13:45. It wasn't as fast as I'd have liked, but it was still four hours faster than our first Ironman the year before.

In January 1988, after a year of racing to include one Ironman, a half Ironman, three Olympic-distance triathlons, five marathons (including one in Barbados), three half-marathons, and fifteen short road races, I wrote a letter to the Hawaii Ironman officials to get permission to compete in the 1988 event. We hadn't won our age division at Hyannis, but I hoped that with our strong performance, we might still get a special invitation from the Hawaii Ironman committee. In my letter, I detailed our race history and capabilities, highlighting our performances in Penticton and Hyannis. I emphasized our experience and passion for the sport and what we could bring to a worldwide event. Finally, I wrote about the honor it would be for us to compete in the race.

We were preparing for our eighth consecutive Boston Marathon when the word came back from the Ironman World Championship: Our application had been rejected. The officials were concerned that the swim would be too dangerous for us. I took their response in stride. We had been rejected before, so I hadn't expected this to come easily. I quickly wrote back, emphasizing the safety measures we always take and pointing out that we had swum triathlon distances before in all kinds of waters. We kept busy with races from California to Massachusetts, and it didn't take long for the Ironman Hawaii folks to respond to my second appeal. The answer was the same. They regretted that they couldn't allow us to compete for safety concerns.

That's when I called in the big guns. Judy used the congressional pull she had from her work with congressmen to implement Chapter 766 a few years earlier to convince a Hawaiian senator that our participation in the prominent competition would be good publicity for his home state. He agreed and got in touch with the Ironman representative in charge of our application, Valerie Silk. At the same time, Dave McGillivray, who had close ties with Ironman committee members, pleaded our case, too. Eventually and incredibly, Silk consented. We were officially invited to participate in the 1988 Ironman World Championship. The invitation came with a warning, however. Silk reiterated that the race would be difficult and that we would likely encounter physical and mental obstacles we had never faced before. That wasn't about to stop us. We were Hawaii bound.

Having raced in warmer climates and taxing terrain before, we knew that we would need extra time to acclimate and adjust to a very different environment. It's not every day we swim against rough ocean current, bike over crumbling lava-covered ground, or run on the hot pavement in the tropics. The trip itself would be challenging. First, we had to account for all our equipment. Getting organized and checking an inflatable boat, bike, and running chair for flying was an ordeal in and of itself. It was always hard on Rick to travel somewhere so far away. He would be very uncomfortable, confined for so long in a plane. Anytime we traveled together, I would constantly check on him, because his tight muscles caused him to slide down in the seat, no matter what kind of restraints were across his lap. I would have to lift him up in his seat regularly to resituate him. With the time difference between Massachusetts and Hawaii, it would completely throw off Rick's habits, from taking his muscle relaxer pills to scheduling bathroom breaks. It would be a trial, but we sensed that getting to Hawaii and being able to compete in such a prestigious event would be worth it. We were right.

We flew to Hawaii ten days before the Ironman World event. Since it was our first time in Hawaii, for the first few days we played tourist, settling in and taking in the sights of the island and adjusting to the warm climate. Our entire family came with us, including Rick's brothers. Rob had gotten married a few months earlier to his childhood sweetheart Mary Conners, and both joined us in Hawaii. I continued my strict training schedule and practiced swimming in the ocean current and biking when the Hawaiian winds were at their strongest. One day, Rob and Russ joined Rick and me on a family swim. We did the whole 2.4 miles together. As the day of the event neared, everyone in the family was excited to see us perform.

At orientation, Ironman reps stressed the importance of hydrating. They also warned that we shouldn't make any last-minute changes to our regular training routine. I got the first part down pat. If only I had listened to the second.

When race day finally arrived, I was filled with emotion. To be out there at 7:00 a.m. in the deep ocean water, surrounded by the greatest triathletes in the world, the sun just coming up, and waiting in the waves for that cannon to go off was incredibly exciting. Rick, stretched out on his beanbag in the inflatable boat, loved it too. I stayed clear of the nearly two thousand other participants by positioning us at the perimeter of the group. Then the cannon fired, and we were off—a mass of swimmers frothing the ocean with our strokes. We had two hours and fifteen minutes to complete the swim course without being disqualified. We made it to the halfway turn in less than an hour. I felt pretty good at that point, but my stomach was a little upset. Not long after, I realized why.

I had made the critical mistake that race representatives had warned us about. I had changed my training routine. Everywhere I had turned, Gatorade reps had been handing out free bottles of their product. (Gatorade was sponsoring the event.) I had never drunk Gatorade before a race and certainly never as my chief source of water. But for whatever reason, I had kept thinking about orientation and staying hydrated, so I must have had a gallon of Gatorade replacement fluid the night before and several more swigs that morning of the event. I didn't know that you should only drink this replacement fluid during the competition or after the event, not before the event starts. The overkill of sugary electrolytes hit me after an hour of swimming.

I cramped up, which I had never done before, and when I swallowed salty ocean water just trying to stay afloat, I vomited up blue-green liquid. We kept trying to swim until the cutoff time expired. Then the crew on the safety boat saw that I was in trouble and safely towed Rick and me back to shore. It was enormously disappointing. I felt I had let everyone down, including myself. I could no longer say that we had finished every race we had ever started. When we got to shore, I had the urge to jump back in the ocean and swim home to Massachusetts. Not surprisingly, my family rallied around me. More surprising, however, was that the next day, when I met with Valerie Silk and the Ironman World race director, Debbie Baker, they encouraged us to try again the following year. They had every confidence we could do it. And we did.

All that next year, I trained harder than I had ever trained before, increasing the amount of time I spent in the water and on the bike. Everything fell perfectly into place. We had found gracious sponsors—American Airlines and XRE—and the Konoloa Hotel in Hawaii put us up for free. All I had to do was pull through on the physical end. (I avoided any liquids except water before the race.)

The 1989 Ironman World Championship in Kona was a race to remember. That morning, we finished the swim in one hour and fifty-four minutes. The wind cutting in from the mountains on the bike leg had proved challenging. But Rick and I were both well-prepared, coated in sunblock and wearing helmets, should we tumble. We finished in under eight hours. The marathon was grueling. I've never been so hot while running. But what an awesome experience it was to approach the finish line. With that crowd at the end, announcers calling out our arrival, and my adrenaline flowing, it was a moment to be truly elated at what we had accomplished.

I knew the credit went to my son. He was my motivation. Something gets into me when I'm competing along with Rick that makes us go faster. My strength comes from him, as if it moves from his body into mine. The strength that I got from my son that day enabled us to become Ironmen.

ABC had covered the entire event and got some great film footage of Rick and me along the route. When it aired, the response was tremendous and touching. At one point, a commentator commented on Rick and me crossing the finish line to a wildly cheering crowd, thrown leis, and tearful family members: "Twenty-seven years ago, the Hoyt family began the long journey that has led to this day and to this moment. Along the way, the family has faced reality squarely. Through love, they have transformed a life of deprivation into a life of possibility."

I then realized we had been handed a wonderful gift, not only the gift of joy a son brings to his father, whatever the child's capabilities, but also the opportunity to spread awareness about persons with disabilities, about what you can achieve if you simply put your mind to it. In the words of Ironman's founding director, Commander John Collins, we had finished what we had started.

The following months brought more TV interviews, articles, and a nomination for Athlete of the Year, which the writer Gerry Callahan in the *Boston Herald* urged be upgraded to Athlete of the Decade. I was humbled and honored. I had simply been grateful for the opportunity to compete with the best and finish. After 1989, we would complete one more Ironman World Competition in Kona, Hawaii—in 1999. No one had ever done the Hawaii Ironman like Team Hoyt. Before us, none had tried the event as a team. To this day, no one has ever towed another person in the swim portion. There have been guides for the legally blind, but the blind athlete swims, bikes, and runs on his or her own with a tether to the guide. Rick and I were unique.

As my fiftieth birthday approached, I knew we had so much more in us. There were many more milestones in our future. What else, I wondered, could Rick and I do, beyond being Ironmen?

Chapter 14

Milestones

O nce we officially became Ironmen, I thought why stop there? Years earlier, it had become clear that this was what we were meant to do, my son and I embarking on adventures together. The more physical the adventure, the better. We were up for almost any competitive challenge that presented itself. We had something to prove. I was a middle-aged man determined to never give up on my firstborn son. Rick, through his entire life, had faced adversity that those of us fortunate enough to be able-bodied cannot imagine. If a 2.4-mile swim in the ocean followed by a 112-mile bike ride (and a marathon-length run after that) didn't get the better of us, nothing could. If we had had the time and the training, we would have climbed Mt. Everest, Rick and I had that much adrenaline and passion for trying new things.

After racing for more than ten years, Rick wasn't a tagalong. He was the star. Rick and I looked at every race—whether a 5K, a marathon, or a triathlon—not as an obstacle to be overcome but as an exciting challenge that had the potential to bring us closer together, just for having finished. With over a decade of competitive racing under our belts, we looked forward to what the future would hold. We had conquered Canada and bested Hawaii. We were Ironmen. What else could we possibly tackle?

The 1980s flew by in a whirlwind. Leading up to and following the Ironman, we competed on home turf, as usual, running marathons and finishing triathlons across the Northeast. In Washington, D.C., we were named to the Honors Court by the Vince Lombardi Tournament of Champions, where we met famous folks like Patrick Ewing, Bob Hope, and Mike Ditka. I shook hands with Bob Hope, and we joked about our golf game. Rick and I won a Healthy American Fitness Leaders (HAFL) Award and got to see the sights in Long Beach, California, when they flew us out for the ceremony. We even took on several half Ironman races, including the Milwaukee half Ironman, although officials nixed the swim portion due to dangerous conditions.

Our travels took us overseas when, in the midst of one Massachusetts winter, we headed for warmer waters when invited to race in Barbados. Though our first Ironman World Championship didn't turn out quite as we had hoped, we had come back strong the next year and felt like chiefs of the island. We followed that with the El Salvador National Triathlon, where the director awarded us two gold medals and a machete for finishing the race.

That race was a cultural experience. The reception we received was heartwarming, considering the poverty we saw and how clear it was that the people in the area had little to cheer about. I have the machete on display in my home, and it always reminds me of our travels and puts things in perspective if ever I'm feeling sorry for myself. I know how lucky I am to be able to do everything that I do and have children who love me and friends who respect me.

All this trekking had gotten me thinking. We had been so many places and had visited states and foreign lands far removed from Massachusetts. We had flown across the United States and back to participate in so many races I had begun to lose track. I would have to consult our records to name them all. We had clocked so many miles in separate states. Why not make it official and race across America? And why not do it in the name of people with disabilities to help raise awareness?

Originally, my big plan was to do a continuous mega-triathlon of sorts. I would swim, run, and bike across America—with Rick as my partner. The problem, of course, was that it was going to be awfully hard to arrange to be near a body of water for the swim portion every day. Still, we could bike and run the journey. We had been doing that practically every day anyway. We would simply chart a longer course that stretched from the West Coast to the East Coast. It sounded easy enough, and ultimately, it was for a cause greater than personal achievement or self-satisfaction. Thanks, in part, to the national attention we had received because of the Ironman, we had established the Hoyt Fund in 1992. The fund was a charitable organization with the goal of enhancing the lives and mobility of people with disabilities. A nationally documented Trek Across America seemed the perfect way to debut the fund, start raising more public funds, and drum up more support. (In 2005 we changed the fund to the nonprofit Hoyt Foundation, Inc.)

Rick was right there with me, excited about the prospect of a road race across the United States. He was nearing a college degree in special education. His goal had also been to spread the word about how able those with disabilities really are. As he said in interviews, he never cared about racing across the United States just for the sake of being able to say we had done it. What he did care about though was calling attention to our organization. He also wanted to do something that people with disabilities had not done before, to show that anything was possible. The deal was done.

No matter the cost, we were going to make that journey together. It took a lot of planning, negotiating, and securing sponsorships. When there wasn't enough to cover the expense of the trip, Judy and I decided to refinance our home for $70,000. It may have seemed rash, but when I had set my sights on something, I was going to see it through, especially when it meant so much to my son. So, in the summer of 1992, with Russ and Judy following behind in an RV, Rick and I took a month and a half to run and bike almost 3,770 miles cross-country, from Santa Monica to—where else—Boston.

It was a family trip, albeit the most tiring family trip I have ever taken. Russ also came along, which was lucky for us, because he turned out to be such a big help. Rob had to stay home to work and take care of his own family, including my first grandson. We saw a lot along the way. The experience was nothing short of amazing. In Los Angeles, we biked past the shells of buildings burned in the riots earlier that spring resulting from the Rodney King trial. We blistered in the Nevada desert and saw snow coating the mountaintops in Utah. We climbed the Rocky Mountains in only a day and ran through lightning in the plains of Nebraska, where Rick was made an honorary colonel in the National Guard. For the Fourth of July, we were in Peru, Illinois, and were featured live on *Wide World of Sports*. In Washington, D.C., at the foot of the steps of the Lincoln Memorial and without a wheelchair ramp in sight, Russ gathered Rick in his arms and carried him all the way to top of the monument, up all those steps, so he could see the statue of President Lincoln up close and personal. It was glorious, one of the proudest moments I have had watching my children, both of them wonderful young men. Forty-five days and 3,735 miles later we returned home to the beautiful city of Boston.

The adventure was exciting, but there were certainly some scary moments along the way. The walkie-talkies we used to communicate were not always the most reliable, and more than once, the RV nowhere in sight, I took a wrong turn on the bike and got lost in unknown locales. It wasn't like I had a GPS to tell us where to go. We had to rely on old maps and intuition. One day when I wasn't paying close attention to what my body was telling me, I passed out in the heat and came to with Rick and the bike tumbled over next to me. Amazingly, this was one of several close calls we were fortunate to escape without injury. I hadn't anticipated how frigid our early morning wake-up calls would be in the desert, and Rick could hardly eat because his body would get so tight from the cold. High altitudes made it difficult to breathe, forcing us to take more breaks than I would have liked. Heavy rains near Maryland caused the bike tires to hydroplane, and the bike and everyone attached to it went down hard. Rick fell right out on the pavement and split his helmet in two. Incredibly, we were both fine, if a little bruised and shaken for a while. Despite a few upsets, we kept a good pace. When we finally rolled into Boston, slightly ahead of schedule on July 23, oh, was it worth it!

We had accomplished the entire trek without taking a day off, something other long-distance runners and bikers we talked to said was impossible. They all told us to take a day or two off each week during the trek to rest our bodies. They said we would be worn out in twenty days and not be able to finish. I felt that we could do the entire trek in forty-five days without taking a day off, because we would get stronger as we biked and ran each day. That's exactly what happened—forty-five days straight.

As we had neared Boston, there was a reception waiting that trumped any other reception we had experienced. It made all the freezing mornings, the painful blisters, and the aching joints that required nightly massages all worth it. Fans had turned out in droves, and ABC-TV filmed our final jaunt to the harbor. A big sign welcoming us to our beloved city was posted overhead. Raymond Flynn, Boston's mayor, and William Weld, governor of Massachusetts, were both there, speeches at the ready. It was announced that the day would be named Dick and Rick Hoyt Day. Rick was presented the state flag of Massachusetts. To cheers of support, Rick and I made our way to the final destination, the harbor. There, as part of our idea about spreading disability awareness and showing that anything is possible, I brought two oceans together by emptying a champagne bottle we'd filled at the start of our quest with water from the Pacific Ocean into the Atlantic. The next day, the Boston Red Sox were playing a nationally televised game, and Rick and I were invited to speak for a few minutes before the game started. We ran from the Marriott Long Wharf Pier through Boston into Fenway Park and then around the bases before we gave a short, four-minute speech to the crowd. Though we hadn't come close to meeting our million-dollar goal for the Hoyt Fund, we knew we had done something good. We had shown the nation, the world—anyone who was watching or who would hear our story—that disabilities do not have to be limiting.

Back home, Rick, who had been such a good sport throughout our journey, a silent and steady partner, finally got to react to our trek. He had time to reflect and comment on the trip and typed this on his TIC: "I am amazed by the beauty of America, and I am amazed by the beauty of the people we met as we crossed the country. I now understand what the song 'America the Beautiful' is all about. I have a lot more respect for the people who first crossed this country to begin a new life." I could not have said it better. The milestone of trekking across the country is a trip I will never forget.

By the mid-nineties, we had been racing competitively for nearly twenty years. Rick and I had seen and done more things together than any father and son could hope. We had traversed the desert, swum the ocean, and shaken hands with presidents. We had transformed from a spastic quadriplegic and his out-of-shape father into runners, then marathoners, triathletes, and Ironmen. Event T-shirts filled our closets and drawers. We had been honored with awards and medals and keys to the city. We had raced across the United States and had taken a victory lap around the bases of Fenway Park afterward. We had created a bond between us that gave me a reason to keep running. Together, my son and I had accomplished more than I think anyone had ever expected.

On October 11, 2008, we were inducted into the Ironman Hall of Fame at the 2008 Ford Ironman World Championship in Kona. Rick even took the stage to deliver a moving speech he had prepared with the help of his computer. He talked about the milestones we had met over the years, ending his speech with a question that got everyone in the audience laughing and crying: "So, what type of vegetable am I?" Quite frankly, it doesn't get any better than that.

Just as Rick was finishing his speech, a Hawaiian rainstorm came out of nowhere. By the time they'd given out the last award, it was pouring, and big puddles were forming on the ground. Someone gave us a few trash bags to wrap around Rick and his TIC. We got soaked and had to run back to our hotel dodging puddles. But we had just gotten inducted into the Ironman Hall of Fame, so we were smiling and laughing as we ran, accepting handshakes and congratulations along the way.

In 2009, my "vegetable" and I would complete our one-thousandth race, the Boston Marathon. We had planned for that, of course, because we couldn't wait for Boston to be our thousandth.

But back in 1993, with hundreds of races under our belt, there was one thing Rick had yet to finish by himself, an accomplishment achieved all on his own, perhaps the biggest milestone of his life. My eldest son, the boy doctors deemed a vegetable, was poised to graduate from college.

DEAR DICK AND RICK:
In June 2006, several good friends of mine were involved in a terrible car accident. Many died and others were seriously injured. A seven-year-old boy was left paralyzed from the waist down

and had below-the-knee traumatic amputation on one of his legs. One day in July after visiting the young boy in rehab, it occurred to me that he would never walk again. There I sat, drinking beer, wasting away in my middle age. Something had to change.

In what was somewhat of a Forrest Gump moment, I put on my running shoes and decided I'd run for the two of us, the young boy and myself. He couldn't run, so I did. One mile became two and two became three. The young boy in my heart kept me running on even the coldest days and days when I had a million excuses not to run.

As the weeks went by I continued to add distance, averaging six miles a day by September. A colleague of mine, who was also a runner, heard about my venture and suggested I run a half-marathon with him in Toronto. With slight apprehension, I agreed and continued training.

Within the week, and at the perfect time, I received a video e-mail from a close friend about a father-son team who was accomplishing the unbelievable. When I saw you two running across the finish line, Rick with the biggest smile on his face, I knew that running the half-marathon was just the beginning for me. I began to train harder. Your story provided me with even more motivation and confidence to complete the race. I knew that if a father could lead his son in so many marathon and triathlon events, I could run a measly 13.1 miles.

Closer to the race, I encountered a soleus strain in my leg and began physical therapy while continuing to train for the half-marathon. It was painful at first, but I constantly thought about the two of you and how difficult it must be sometimes for you, Dick, as you are reaching the twenty-six–mile marker in your marathons, pushing that extra body. You do it though, because you love Rick and want him to be happy. I knew I had to keep going for my young friend.

I finished the half-marathon on October 15, 2006, in less than two hours! It truly was a once-in-a-lifetime experience among four thousand other runners. But I knew I could do more.

On Sunday, May 20, 2007, I ran for you. With your inspiration, I accomplished more than I ever dreamed and ran my first marathon. With great support from my family and friends, I raised more than $1,000 for the Hoyt Foundation, Inc., and beat my personal marathon goal by almost twenty-two minutes, logging a time of 3:38.58. Not bad for a guy who started running July 2006 at forty-one years old. I ran for Team Hoyt, I ran for the foundation, and I ran for my buddy who would never walk again.

"Mercy Me"—the same song featured in your YouTube video—was my power song during the race. This song was a simple reminder as I ran, of the support that the two of you give to each other. Running my marathon was an emotional experience. It had nothing to do with me physically, but I carried with me the emotion that I had for the two of you and for the nine-year-old boy who was paralyzed. I'm sure people thought I was crazy. As I listened to the Mercy Me song on my iPod, streams of tears fell down my cheeks and pictures of you, Rick and my little friend, filled my mind. Nobody had a clue of my story. I ran by the other runners with the word *CAN* written on an index card pinned to my back, forgetting about anyone else running that day. It has been two years since my first marathon, and I still have not run as fast as I did in that race.

After I completed that marathon, I downloaded a copy of your YouTube video and keep it on my BlackBerry as motivation to get me through each day. I show your video to anyone I come across who may need inspiration. I'll bring it out when I engage in a conversation about my triathlons and running, or even in a business meeting if the situation seems appropriate. I always tell people if you want to find a really inspiring story, look up Team Hoyt.

Team Hoyt has inspired me not only in my running, but in my family life as well. I am lucky enough to have my kids healthy, running around playing soccer, and here you are, Dick, devoting the majority of your life to provide for Rick so that he can experience things he otherwise wouldn't have the opportunity to. Many parents in your situation fear for what might happen to their children if they aren't careful, shielding them from realities. Because of you, Rick has lived a life chock-full of love and excitement. Even though my situation isn't as challenging as your own, I now strive to be a better father to my children.

With Team Hoyt continuing to inspire me, I have done several Olympic distance triathlons over the last couple of years, and I just signed up for my first half Ironman for next year. You guys have made me push myself in directions I would never have imagined ten years ago.

Thank you,
DAVID CHIPPI
AVON LAKE, OHIO

Chapter 15

Rick's Independence

O n May 16, 1993, Rick and I found ourselves at a packed Nickerson Field. The rest of the family was there as well— Rick's brothers, several of my siblings, Judy, and over five thousand student participants. It was a beautiful spring day, and the air was filled with anticipation. Reporters swarmed and cameras flashed. The rumbling crowd finally quieted as a man made his way across a small stage to a podium to deliver his welcoming remarks. This wasn't the start of another race; it was the end of one. Nine years in the making, it was a challenge Rick had faced and conquered all by himself. This was Boston University's one hundred twentieth commencement ceremony, and my eldest son was graduating with a degree in special education.

That day in 1993, at the age of thirty-one, Rick became the first nonspeaking quadriplegic to ever graduate from the School of Education at Boston University. He became one of the first nonspeaking, quadriplegic students to graduate from *any* university. And he graduated with a B average. He had accomplished this amazing achievement all on his own, without any favors or special treatment. I could not have been prouder on that day. It was by far one of the best days of my life.

Several newspapers covered his graduation, including the *Boston Herald* and the *Boston Globe*. Even *Hard Copy*, the television program, was present for the event. We were touched by articles with headlines like "Graduating to success," "Tenacity's his way of life," and "Triumph! Special BU student goes this marathon alone—and wins." It was Rick's day. Rick summed it up best, when he told one reporter, "I can't compare the marathons to my graduation. I feel just great. Overall great. Euphoric." His euphoria was contagious. The graduation and the degree were a long time coming. In true Hoyt fashion, it had not been an easy road.

Though it may have seemed that racing took over our lives, we had plenty of other things going on as well and were meeting milestones left and right—outside the running world. By the early nineties, both Rob and Russ had gotten married and started families and careers of their own. Judy had finished her graduate degree, and I was still working for the National Guard. It wasn't always easy to balance such a hectic life. As we would eventually discover firsthand, that hectic lifestyle wasn't cut out for everyone. My relationship with Judy was suffering from the toll of Rick and me racing every weekend and spending all our spare time training for those races.

On the heels of marathons, triathlons, and cross-country trips, with Rick just entering adulthood, it was clear that races were important to my family, but they also had to fit within our full schedules. A large part of that full schedule had included Rick attending college and living independently, a huge endeavor that few could have predicted for him. I always hoped the best for Rick, no matter what the experts told us. As the years went by, I was happy to see them proved wrong. It was a joy to see my child all grown up and participating in life like any other young man.

In 1984, almost a decade since he had been admitted to public school, Rick had graduated from Westfield High School. It had been a big year for him. It was our first year to compete as official entrants in the Boston Marathon. Rick had a date to the senior prom. We had shaken the hands of political dignitaries and sports superstars. No event in 1984 was quite so momentous, however, as his high school graduation. Rick had worked so hard to finish his studies. After all the effort it took just to get him into the public school system, we couldn't have been happier with the outcome. Everyone was rooting for Rick that day. When his name was called, he received a standing ovation. It was an emotional moment. Judy and I and the rest of his friends and family were pleased as punch to see Rick being pushed across the stage to "Pomp and Circumstance" and receiving his diploma, presented by the mayor of Westfield.

I would have been proud had he decided to stop his schooling there, but Rick is not one to settle for average. He was college bound, and there wasn't anything stopping him. Like any high school graduate, he had a mind and desires of his own. We had even quibbled over his choice of college. Though initially I would have preferred to have him closer to home, at Westfield State, I knew Rick was ready for more independence and freedom. So I wasn't surprised that he had set his sights on Boston University. Judy tried to get him to go to the University of Massachusetts at Amherst, where she'd received her special education degree, but Rick was determined to move to the city and attend the private university on the banks of the Charles River. BU was a great school, consistently ranked top in the nation for its excellent occupational therapy and biomedical engineering programs, areas of study which, of course, had been important to Rick growing up. Like his mother, he had his heart set on special education and looked forward to being at the other end of the spectrum to find ways to help people in situations similar to his own.

After Judy and I relented, there was just one thing standing in my son's way—the welfare department had denied funds for his personal care assistants. The way the Boston Center for Independent Living (BCIL) saw it, since Rick couldn't speak, he would be unable to tell a PCA what his needs were. Judy and I knew otherwise. He'd been telling us what to do for years! So Rick and his mother went straight to the welfare department where they presented their case—and stayed until they won their hearing. We weren't about to have our son once again denied the opportunity of an education. Ultimately, Rick was allotted the same funding from the state's Rehabilitation Commission to attend the private university that it would have offered him had he chosen a state college. This battle, thankfully, was much more easily won than getting Rick into public school. All it took was for Rick to speak for himself. He demonstrated his TIC and, in case that wasn't enough, explained his brother Russ's system of communicating with him. We were in, or rather, Rick was in—to Boston University.

With impending statewide budget cuts that threatened to do away with the benefit of PCAs entirely, Judy spent more time with legislators and took Rick's example to those in charge of implementing the bill on disabilities and showed them the kind of care the disabled could receive. She explained that it would cost the state a whole lot less to bill Medicaid for PCAs, who at that time got paid $8 an hour, than it would to support Rick in an institution. Securing health care funding is never easy, but we have been fortunate that Rick has had such good care over the years—critical to not only his independence, but his daily survival.

Fortunately for Rick, he was granted the means to attend the college of his choice. In the fall of 1984, Judy, his brothers, and I packed Rick up and moved him to Boston. He was officially a college man. That ride back to Westfield after dropping Rick off at college was bittersweet. It brought to mind the long ride home from the specialist the day we were told exactly what was wrong with Rick. Only this time, we were filled with hope and expectations. Any good parent feels sad when he realizes that his child no longer needs him. We felt that times twenty. At the same time, it was more than I could have ever hoped for my son.

With the help of caretakers, Rick lived on his own, staying in the dorms like any other college kid. Of course, he had to have nearly around-the-clock assistance from his PCAs—mostly other students—but he was away from home and experiencing adulthood, without his worried parents looking over his shoulder every minute. If he was homesick, he sure didn't let on to us about it. Rick loved college, and everyone seemed to love having him there. Any time

I would visit or whenever we would get together for races, it was clear that Rick was a big man on campus. His new friends often showed up to cheer us on when we competed. Some were even moved to take up the sport themselves.

During his first year in the dorm, Rick lived on the same floor as the BU hockey team. He loved that, even though it could get rowdy—probably because it *did* get rowdy. He told me how the hockey team "borrowed" an ice statue and hid it in the dorm's communal bathroom. It was the middle of winter, so to keep it from melting, they left all the windows open, just to see how long the statue would hold its form. Rick got a real kick out of that one. The freezing temperatures didn't bother him because he was used to withstanding inclement weather during all those cold mornings when we raced.

Another time, Rick found himself stranded in a bathroom, only this time it was the women's bathroom. His dorm was coed, but the men and women stayed on different floors. Some of the other guys pulled a prank on Rick in the middle of the night, zipped him up in the sleeping bag he always slept in, and snuck him up to the ninth floor and left him stranded in the women's bathroom in his long johns. If I didn't know better, I'd say Rick managed to sneak up there himself. He's determined enough when he wants something.

Rick got along great with his caretakers, some of whom were real characters. For the most part, they were wonderful. We recently received a letter from a woman, now a lawyer in New York, who was one of Rick's PCAs in Boston. She joked that when she was under drinking age, Rick was able to get her into bars since she was his caretaker and they'd have to let her in to accompany him. Now she's a lawyer for people with disabilities. Her experience with Rick encouraged her to become, not a corporate lawyer, but an attorney who represents those who need it most.

When Rick was in college, though, sometimes the stories I would hear after the fact are better left untold. I recognize that it was a lot to ask of someone to watch out for my son, an especially big task to ask of young adults, but the caretaking didn't always go smoothly. For example, one night when Rick was staying in the dorms, one of his PCAs didn't show up. So Rick sat there all night long with no pills, no supper, no bathroom break. He wasn't discovered until the next morning, when his roommate came in after a long night out. Rick couldn't do anything in that situation because he can't talk or pick up the telephone. He was stuck.

Making sure someone was there for him at all times was always one of our greatest concerns. Most of his PCAs were other college students, just doing what college students do. They'd go out drinking, have a good time, and forget. It was pretty nerve-racking, without a family member close to go check on him. I always told his PCAs, if they were not going to show up, at least call another PCA to make sure the shift was covered. If they couldn't find someone, they were to call me. I used to get a lot of those phone calls. I made quite a few trips to the city. I didn't mind. I welcomed any excuse to visit my son.

Usually, those visits weren't for anything major. Rick would always say, in that I'm-too-old-for-this, college kid manner, "I'm fine, Dad. What are you doing here?" Then we'd wind up going out for dinner or simply having a good talk to catch up. It gave us an opportunity to plan upcoming races and discuss how they were going to fit into Rick's school schedule. Because of the distance, this meant that we could not train together on a daily basis. I worked out at the gym, ran, swam, and biked on my own.

Let's be honest—those visits to Boston were more for my benefit than my son's.

One scary situation, however, left me wondering if college was such a good idea after all. As you have probably surmised, Rick is the life of any party. He's a fun guy to be around, a continual prankster. If his PCAs wanted to go out to the bars at night, they often took Rick along with them. One night, he was outside a bar with one of his PCAs, minding his own business, when someone tried to attack them. The PCA got knocked around a little, and Rick wound up on the ground. I think the guys who did it were probably drunk, recognized Rick from the Boston Marathon, and felt like giving him a hard time for whatever reason. I didn't know what happened until the next day when I got the call from our good friend, Eddie Burke, who lived in Waltham and was also our go-to guy in case of emergency. Eddie had taken Rick home that night. Rick was a little shaken up, but physically okay. Fortunately, that's the only time I think Rick ever thought he was going to get harmed. For him, the trade-off—to be able to attend college and hang out with other college-aged kids—was worth any danger.

Rick was busy enjoying college life, and it didn't take long for word to get out about him going to BU. In a TV show that aired on the CBS *Evening News*, Meredith Vieira interviewed us because she said she had to see it to believe it. She came to the house when Rick was home for a break, saw how we fed and took care of him, and then followed him back to Boston. She even hung out in the bars with Rick and his friends.

Vieira reported the story from Rick's point of view, showing the effort it took for him to go to class every day and pursue a college degree. For example, it took him six times the amount of studying that it took other students. That meant he could only manage two courses every semester, but that didn't stop Rick. He was determined to get a degree, without any special favors. She asked Rick, "What's so important about living independently?" Rick typed out this response on his computer: "If I can't live independently, then I want to die." That took us all by surprise. But I think it shows how important independence really is to Rick, and how hard he's willing to work to maintain it. When Vieira left, I think she was surprised by all that Rick had accomplished, to see him living his dream and attending college. A few years later, she sent us a nice donation. She had a relative who was facing a similar disability, so the story hit close to home. She was amazed by the work he was doing, both at BU and in the rest of life.

Between school and athletics, Rick was living the life. He loved listening to music (among his favorites: AC/DC and Queen), going to university sporting events, and hanging out with friends at the local hot spots. Rick even joined the intramural swim team. But like many students, the temptations of college life nearly compromised all he was working toward. Rick was not immune to the effects of peer pressure or the desire to simply check out from all the challenges he faced on a daily basis. He admitted in interviews that he didn't take his first few years at BU quite as seriously as he perhaps should have. There was too much of a good time to be had on his own. Who could blame him?

There comes a time, though, in every young man's life when he has to be honest with himself. For Rick, the honest truth came totally unexpectedly. He came home from college for a visit and told me, "Dad, I think I'm an alcoholic." The pressures of school had gotten to him, and more often than not he found himself in the bars, drinking too much. His drink of choice? Rum and Coke—and his friends and PCAs obliged. He's a hard guy to say no to. It was the same situation that affects most kids when they go off to college. Mom and Dad are not around, they are able to do what they want, so instead of studying, they hit the bars to party and drink. Of course Rick's mom and I were upset when he told us, but Rick assured us that he would cut down on his drinking and partying and start concentrating on his schoolwork, which he did. Fortunately in our case, our son took care of the situation himself, and everything was fine after that.

About midway through his college experience, Rick buckled down, got serious, and moved into a quiet dorm where he could focus on his studies. It took nine years of hard work on his part—Rick used to joke with university officials that when he finally graduated and the school was no longer receiving his tuition, they'd all be in for a world of hurt. To me, it seemed as if I had snapped my fingers, and suddenly there was another college graduate in the family.

Before the Boston University commencement ceremonies, Rick was honored by the university president, John Silber. Silber talked about how inspiring Rick had been to others, how he challenged all kinds of students to reevaluate their own capabilities and try harder to do better. He talked specifically about the work Rick had invested in his education, how he had gone it alone because he wanted to show what he could do without special assistance. Finally, he told the audience that they would soon have the pleasure of saying they graduated with Rick Hoyt. Rick even got the chance to address his classmates and thank the university, when his PCA and closest friend for the final four years of college, Neil Danilowicz, wheeled Rick onto the stage and then went to the microphone to deliver a few words that Rick had written earlier.

Graduation was a success well-earned by a man most doctors had said would never live to see this day, let alone take part in it in such an integral way. This was Rick's time to shine. It was his accomplishment, and one of my proudest moments being his father. My son had plans and he had a future, which was all I could have ever wished for him. As Rick smartly told anyone who would listen, he planned on spending his extra time "looking for a job, an apartment, and a wife."

After Rick graduated from college, he continued living on his own and started a job at Boston College. He was consulting with engineers in a program called Eagle Eyes, in which he was helping them develop a new augmentative communication device for people with disabilities. It was pretty cool stuff. They were basically trying to come up with something that tracked eye movement, so that a person could use his or her eyes like a computer mouse in order to communicate. As he has always done since he was just a little boy, he was helping others. I was extremely proud. Rick was a working man, living independently.

For someone like Rick, though, every day can be filled with a new set of dangers. Even the best PCAs came to learn that. One of Rick's favorite PCAs, Heather Omans, took the job as his caretaker after he graduated from BU and went to work for Boston College. She was loading him up in the van to take him to work one day and had him nearly to the top of the lift when, without her noticing, his wheelchair brakes unlocked. Instead of rolling forward into the van, he rolled straight out—and to the ground three feet below. He fell flat on his face and broke his nose. Luckily, that was the extent of his injuries, but it sure scared poor Heather.

Later, Heather told me that when she saw him lying there on the ground, his face bloodied, she'd been terrified that she would have to explain to me how she'd killed my son. At the hospital, she told Rick she'd been afraid that he had suffered brain damage because of the fall. Rick, thankfully, was fine—just a little worse for wear. Hooked up to his TIC, he had recovered well enough to type, "That's ok. I already have brain damage." I still laugh when I think of his attitude about the whole thing. He gave Heather a good ribbing about it from time to time, even joking that if she was ever looking for a second profession, she might consider becoming a mortician. Neither of us held it against her. How could we? I'd had my own share of accidents involving Rick. He's a pretty tough guy, and a few scrapes and bruises weren't going to dampen his spirit.

Another time, though, Rick had an even closer call. It's a miracle he made it out okay. Ever since college, Rick has lived independently, with the help of his caretakers, but he doesn't have a PCA stay with him at night. He sleeps alone in his apartment. To avoid getting bed sores that come from lying in one position without being able to move around, he used to sleep on a waterbed. One night not long after the broken nose incident, the bed sprang a leak, and there he was, lying face down on it. No one was there to check on him in the middle of the night. Rick later told us that when he realized what was happening, that he might likely drown in his own bed, he prayed for God to save him. Soon after, there was a knock on the door, and someone entered the apartment. It was the on-duty night maintenance man, and for whatever reason, he decided to use his master key to go in. It was highly unusual for him to have done that, but as he stood outside Rick's apartment, he had gotten an overwhelming feeling that something was wrong. He got there just in time to get Rick out of the soggy bed and to safety.

Rick's belief in God was strengthened that night. He approached Heather, a Mormon, to learn more about her religion. She introduced him to a couple of Mormon missionaries, who talked with him about their faith. One had a brother with a disability, so they bonded. Rick told us that the doctrine that ultimately drew him to the church was the idea that when we are resurrected, our bodies are perfect. That appealed to him. In 1997, Rick was baptized in the Mormon faith.

Just a few years earlier, our entire family was there to witness Rick's milestone achievement of graduating from college and starting his life as an independent adult. However, we were not to stay the same family unit much longer. A month prior to Rick's graduation, right before the Boston Marathon, Judy had announced in a letter to our family that she no longer wished to be married to me. It was certainly a difficult blow, given all that we had been through with Rick—and then to see him turn out such a success, a college graduate—but sometimes, life happens that way. After Rick's graduation, Judy and I went our separate ways. For the first time, I started seriously considering how I wanted to spend the rest of my life. Rick was a college graduate, living and working on his own. It was time for me to make a few changes myself.

TEAM HOYT,

My son Kevin has three posters hanging in his bedroom, one of Muhammad Ali, one of Dick Butkus, and the last is of Team Hoyt. Kevin is a fifteen-year-old sports fanatic who just so happens to have cerebral palsy. Like Rick, due to complications in the delivery process, oxygen and blood flow were cut off between Kevin and his mother, causing him to be born without a heartbeat and not breathing. Kevin has come a long way since then and through the inspiration of you and Rick, he has surpassed boundaries that many people thought would never be crossed.

About five years ago, my family and I picked up your book, *It's Only a Mountain*. Since Kevin was very young, he has loved sports. We were always out running in his jogger, and we had him involved in an assortment of wheelchair sports, but nothing like the activities in your book. Each night we would read a little bit and we became more and more excited because of the amazing things that you and Rick were accomplishing. Your story inspired our family not only in the athletic sense, but there were also some chapters that we felt we had already read because we related so closely. There's an inherent connection with you because your family has crossed a lot of the same bridges, many more than we have, however. You have cut a path for those of us who are dealing with similar challenges you dealt with early on.

When we finished the last chapter, I remember looking at Kevin and telling him that we would meet you and Rick some day. About three months later, Kevin's physical therapy group was having a fund-raiser and I thought it was the perfect time. When I suggested we reach out to you guys, I never expected to get a positive response. After Kevin and I picked you up from the airport, we knew that there was a connection and that we would definitely be seeing more of you. Just talking to you, we hit it off so well, that it felt like we knew each other. It's remarkable how when you share similar struggles and experiences with someone, an instant connection can be made.

After stepping up our game in the running world, we actually had our chance to run with the Team Hoyt in Virginia Beach for the 2007 half-marathon. Kevin and I have this challenge between us that we are actually going to keep up with you guys in a race someday. I say that we'll have to wait until you are ninety-five, Dick. I'm just kidding, but I think Kevin is serious about it.

Now that Kevin is almost sixteen years old, his independence is thriving. He doesn't want his dad helping him through things. The device that we use to run together is actually a bike that I've adapted that I can push like a jogger, but Kevin is actually the one pedaling on the bike and steering. When we began using it, he could barely get it down the driveway. Now we go out for bike rides, and as long as it's flat or downhill he's fine. Eventually he wants to ride completely on his own.

Another example of Kevin's independence was shown when he competed in several races independently using his walker. His first 5K was done with the Achilles track club where many special needs children and some disabled athletes were present. One athlete in particular was present, Scott Rigsby, the first double amputee to compete in an Ironman Triathlon. By the end of the race, the entire crowd was walking the final loop and cheering for Kevin. When he crossed the finish line, Mary Bryant, the director of the Achilles Track Club, was waiting for him with a special award, and Rigsby gave him his plaque expressing the inspiration he received from Kevin.

The following year, the Achilles Track Club called us and wanted Kevin to come up to Central Park and compete in their five-mile run. He completed it in probably two-and-a-half hours. The whole time I was helping him visualize you pushing Rick in the Ironman, pulling him through the water, completing thirty some odd Boston Marathons, running all over the world, and we talked about it during the whole race. We kept thinking how much harder it would be if we were competing against you guys. Kevin just kept on going. We used you as motivation.

When he finished those five miles, there were so many tears in the crowd, including mine. I can only imagine the reach that you guys have. I don't think you could possibly comprehend the caliber of impact you have on a family like ours.

Like Rick, Kevin plans to go on to college after high school. His goal is to attend Georgia Tech to earn a degree in engineering and work on devices that will help the handicapped. I don't think you get the credit you deserve when it comes to the educational realm. Without your family, this dream of Kevin's would not be plausible.

The two worlds that you guys have pursued in Rick's life are such a great combination. I know that Kevin has the independent drive to accomplish everything that Rick has, but without you two, I don't know if he would have been able to conceptualize it. He has it in his head that he can do anything himself, and he won't give up his goal of a half-marathon with you and Rick.

Thank you for inspiring me daily,
RICH ENNERS
ATLANTA, GEORGIA

Chapter 16

My Military Career

With Rick's busy calendar, I made sure to maximize the time we spent together. We kept racing—hadn't stopped since 1977—but we were both still balancing our racing schedule with jobs and other obligations. Judy had moved out and would file for divorce by the end of 1993, so I was left on my own at the lake house. It gave me a lot of time to think. Surrounded by our family photos, the ribbons and paraphernalia, and memories of all the races we had competed in was sometimes bittersweet. In many ways, the evidence of our accomplishments was proof of the time we had spent together as a family unit. It wasn't only me and Rick out there all those years. We had had a strong support system backing us, and despite the differences that eventually drove us apart, my soon-to-be ex-wife was a part of that. It was a big change for me and a lot to grow accustomed to. The solitude got me thinking about making some more changes in my life.

In terms of racing, I kept busier than ever, training for Ironman races, marathons, and triathlons. In 1994, we even fulfilled a longtime dream of mine and flew to Japan to compete, not in Ironman Japan, but the next best thing: the Tokunoshima Triathlon. The island was gorgeous, just as I had always dreamed Japan would be, complete with lush rice fields, hilly countryside, ancient buildings, and crystal clear water that reminded me of Kona and the Hawaii Ironman. Everywhere we went, the people of Tokunoshima gave us flowers, and we felt incredibly welcome in such a faraway land. It more than compensated for the pain of jet lag and the discomfort of adjusting to the Japanese raw diet, the latter of which produced some rather unfortunate side-effects during the bike leg of the triathlon. I recovered though, and we crossed the finish line—once again, not in last place—to the warm welcome of the Japanese spectators.

When we got home from that adventure, I reflected on the once-in-a-lifetime trip I had been so fortunate to go on. As ever, it was good to be back on home turf, but I sensed more new adventures on the horizon. My family was moving forward, in various directions, to new careers and new starts of their own. It occurred to me that maybe I should consider using the isolation as an opportunity. At fifty-three, I wasn't getting any younger, and I knew that despite what Rick and I had achieved so far in the racing world and the wonderful places we had visited, there was still so much we could do. I knew we could do those things in the name of raising disability awareness.

I wanted to be able to focus my energies on competitive racing with my son—as long as I was physically able. The social climate was changing. People were beginning to more readily accept us and seemed interested in hearing our story. It felt like the ideal time to concentrate on improving the lives of others. From the very first race, Rick had had a sense of charitable giving—the kind of message he could send to others facing debilitation or setbacks. At the beginning, however, I had run with my son for selfish reasons. I knew he loved it, and it made me feel good to do something that brought him joy. All those years, it had been a healthy hobby, a way for me to spend my weekends and downtime with my son. Until then, I had been fitting races into my schedule anytime I could. I was still working full-time for the Air National Guard and reporting to the base for duties there. After a weekend of racing, I might be sore the next week at work, but the thrill of competing and knowing how much Rick relished our time together was worth any discomfort.

I had always felt some degree of guilt for not being able to be there for every event in my children's lives, especially Rick's, given the additional challenges he faced day in and day out. Occasionally my absence was unavoidable, of course. I knew that. And I know that all parents face the same dilemma—how to balance a working life with a family life. I had to earn a living to provide for my family. That meant sometimes being absent for milestones I wish I could have been there for. Running, at exactly the right time in all our lives, naturally presented itself as a means for me to make up to Rick for the time that I had missed.

All these years, I had been running for my son. My promise was that I would continue racing, so long as that was what Rick wanted. But as I moved into my fifties and retirement was in sight, I realized that another opportunity was at hand. Thanks to media attention at the bigger races and various nationally syndicated interviews we had done over the years, people knew who we were. They frequently contacted us with their own stories. In all the letters we received, it had become clear that we had a captive audience that could help us potentially make a difference for other people—whether able-bodied or struggling with a disability.

The time had come for me to concentrate on Team Hoyt, to truly make up for any time I had missed with Rick during his youth, but also to respond to a greater calling. I have always loved a hard day's work and still do, but after years of competitive racing with my disabled son, I had a new outlook on work. I was determined to use my personal drive and work ethic to not only continue racing with my son, but also raise awareness of people with disabilities. It was time to retire from my day job and focus on the activity that had been taking up my weekends for almost twenty years.

I'm the kind of guy who always looks to the future and who is ready for the next adventure, but the more I contemplated retirement, the more I realized how influential my military career had been on my racing life. It may have been a relatively run-of-the-mill military experience, but it had prepped me in so many ways to be a better competitor. Given the time that I served in the military, I know I was fortunate that I never had to go into combat and was never shot at or injured. As in the credo of any National Guardsman, I was ready for active duty at any time, but I suppose I got lucky. I was never called upon. Like any other enlisted military guy, I started off pretty low on the totem pole. I had done my share of KP and guard duty. In order to advance, I had gone to school for basic and then advanced training for the army. After graduating from several training programs, I finally went to school for my chosen field: the missile defense program.

Those were the early days, when Rick was just a toddler and our whole lives loomed before us. It was through the missile defense program that I learned how to operate radar systems and spent most of my active duty time on the East Coast, as an air defense radar operator for the Nike Ajax missiles system. During the early part of my career, the Nike missile was upgraded to the Hercules missile, and I upgraded, too, as a radar operator for the Hercules system. Pretty quickly, I was promoted to section chief in charge of the radar systems. Then I became a commissioned officer and was put in charge of the missile launching control area in Lincoln, Massachusetts. My next position in Lincoln was executive officer in charge of the fire control site. I scheduled the crews, made sure they were qualified for the duties they had to perform, and ran the drills. Little did I know at the time that the military mind-set of dedication to duty would help turn me into a committed runner.

After my stint in Lincoln, Massachusetts, I switched from the Army National Guard to the Air National Guard and became the security officer at Otis Air Force Base on Cape Cod. I was responsible for the security force, which was in charge of guarding the planes at the Air Force base. This was when we bought our dream home, though it was to be a short-lived dream. When the whole missile system and the housing of weaponry missiles was determined unnecessary and became obsolete, I was transferred to Westfield, Massachusetts, to Barnes Airport as the administration officer for the base.

As we settled into Westfield and Rick entered school, I settled into my military duties with the Air National Guard. I became chief of personnel, enlisting and testing all the people who joined the Air National Guard at Barnes. For a short time I was transferred to Wellesley, not far away from Westfield, where the headquarters for the Massachusetts Air National Guard was located, and there I served as the director of personnel. Finally, I was sent back to Barnes in Westfield, where I was promoted to executive support officer for the base. I was involved with all the support areas at the base. Perhaps appropriate, given my weekend activities, my additional duties included promoting nonsmoking, physical fitness, and weight control. So, in other words, everyone hated me! I made the enlisted guardsmen quit smoking, lose weight, and work out to stay in shape. It was around this time that Rick first became interested in racing, so this was the perfect job for me. I even organized runs that took place during the workday, which gave me time to get in some training.

I have always been good with my hands and considered myself a craftsman of sorts. But I had stopped doing masonry work around the time that I was transferred to Barnes in Westfield. Before, when I was working on the missile site, I was scheduled for twenty-four hours on, and then got forty-eight hours off, so I had time to work on masonry and other construction projects on the side when I was off-duty. When I was transferred to Westfield, my schedule changed to working five days a week as well as one weekend per month. This, of course, was in addition to our races every weekend, so I had no time left for masonry.

The National Guard was always supportive of my decision to run in races with Rick and gave me time off whenever I needed it. Because I so rarely used it, I accumulated my vacation time and sick time. That made things easier, for instance, when I needed to take longer stretches of time off to travel for a race. I had that extra leave built up. When I took off forty-five days in a row in 1993 to run and bike across the United States, I was able to do so with the guard's blessing. In every state that we entered during our trek, the National Guard met us and presented us with the flag from their state.

If ever we needed equipment for Kamp for Kids or were looking for some impromptu racing rigging, we were welcome to the supplies in storage on base. (Often, in those early days, Rick's racing equipment was pieced together with guard materials.) The way the guard supported our endeavors was pretty special. The people from my base encouraged Rick and me at every new event we entered. I feel fortunate to have had that kind of backing from my employer and fellow guardsmen all those years. In the spirit of that relationship, I started a road race at the base in Westfield. Rick and I ran with a National Guard Marathon Group for quite a few years as well, wearing their team singlet when racing. I was proud to be affiliated with the guard.

Balancing the daily work grind with training and event racing only made me a more dedicated athlete. My hours during the last several years of my military career were ideal for competitive racing. I worked Monday through Friday from 8 a.m. until 4:30 p.m. at the base in Westfield, with a weekend per month required on duty. I was used to keeping a tight schedule, and I functioned best when I had a lot on my plate.

After thirty-five years in the guard, it was a difficult decision to finally retire. The guard had become part of my extended family. I was treated extremely well by both the higher ranking officers and the lower-ranked enlistees who worked for me. For several years in a row, the unit that I headed had been awarded "outstanding unit of the year," which spoke well for the men and women who worked for me, and how well we were able to perform our duties as a group. I feel I performed my job well and that people respected my work ethic. That, along with my achievements in the military, enabled me to retire from the Air National Guard as a lieutenant colonel on July 28, 1995. After thirty-five years of military service, I had to wonder what was next. Between wanting to race as much as possible and spreading awareness about what can be achieved if a person only believes in himself, I had a few things in mind.

People had long been telling me, "Oh, you gotta write a book. It would be so inspirational." I heard it from race spectators, from coworkers, from family members. But between my duties with the guard and racing every spare moment, I had never really had the time. Then I retired. After that, I sat down for six months and tried my hand at writing. I kept thinking to myself, "If you're going to write a book, now's the time to do it." So I put in the time. What I wanted was not so much to tell everyone every detail of my personal history, but to get down Rick's and my story—to use that as a sounding board for our work raising disability awareness. I was determined to use my newfound free time, in retirement, to give back to the community. All I had to do was figure out the best method for reaching as many people as possible with our message—that anything is possible if you only commit to doing it. So in 2005, we did the necessary paperwork to give the Hoyt Fund nonprofit status, and it became the Hoyt Foundation Inc. We started having fundraisers to garner donations and with those donations began helping out at local summer camps for disabled kids, as well as local therapeutic horseback riding organizations.

DEAR DICK AND RICK,

When you become a father, something changes in you, something drives you. Some fathers are driven by fear. Fear of their child becoming ill or being unhappy. For me, I was driven by the absolute need to be a hunter-gatherer type. I wanted my family to drive the biggest car, live in the fanciest house, and go to the best school. To make this happen, I felt like I had to make some sacrifices.

After being medically discharged from the British forces, I returned home and became quite successful in the business world. I was running a large company, and working seven days a week, eighteen hours a day. Being completely entangled in the corporate world, I only compared myself with others in that world. Compared to them, I was doing quite well, but I would return home from work and my six-month-old son wouldn't come to me. He didn't want to be near me because he didn't know who I was. I knew something was wrong, but I didn't know how to change it. I guess I was stuck in the trap that a lot of us find ourselves in.

Like many of my business trips to the United States, after the flight I was jetlagged and up at 3 a.m. watching ESPN. But this time was different. Instead of watching *SportsCenter* for the third time that day, I was watching you and Rick run across the television, racing for the finish line in the 1999 Hawaii Ironman. It was like the lights came on. Here I was thinking I was doing all the right things. I was traveling for business, getting contracts signed and trying to make a better financial life for my two kids, while all this time they were both at home thinking, "Where's Dad?"

The next week, I got off the plane from New York, called up my lawyer, and sold my business. I thought I was doing the right thing by working every hour God sent me, when what I should have been doing is making sure that I was spending enough time with my kids. Rick, if your father could swim 2.4 miles pulling you in a raft behind him, ride 112 miles on a bike rigged to hold you on the front and run 26 miles while pushing you in a racing chair, why was I not even around to toss a ball around in the backyard with my sons? With a complete shift in lifestyle, I was home all the time with my kids, pushing them around on bikes in the street, helping with homework, and making my family my number one priority, with work at the bottom of my list.

You guys also inspired me to begin training for my own Ironman, the 2005 U.K. Ironman. I laced up my trainers and started off. My first time out, I barely made it three miles down the road when I became violently ill and turned back toward home feeling a little embarrassed about my inability. I had a long road ahead of me, so I began an eighteen-month training regiment. My days were perfect. Instead of leaving for work in the early hours of the day and returning after the kids were in bed, I would wake up in the morning, spend time with my children over breakfast, drop them off at school, and have the rest of the day to train.

Everything was going textbook, until the evening of June 21st. Before I went out to dinner with my wife for our anniversary, I decided to take a quick hour bike ride to keep me on track. I was no more than two miles from home when a car going sixty miles per hour came out of nowhere and hit me. My bike was sucked under the car, as I flew into the windshield, over the roof, and went bouncing down the road. My injuries were intense, but fixable. I fractured my elbow, my ulna in four places, two fingers, was bruised everywhere and had stitches all the way down one leg and on my shoulder. To top it all off, my bike was mangled.

I knew I would be okay, but my trip to the hospital brought on the reality I wanted to avoid. I remember asking the surgeon if

I could compete in the Ironman six weeks later. He just laughed. After all of the hard work I put in, my goal had become out of reach.

After about two weeks full of ill-tempered behavior on my part, a friend of mine who had been training with me came over with the inspiration I needed. He knew that you and Rick had been my motivation for the changes in my life and my desire to complete an Ironman, so he ordered a copy of the 1999 Hawaii Ironman off the Internet and brought it over. I put the DVD in and remember thinking if you guys can do it with more of a disability than just a broken arm, I guess I can too. And that's what I did.

Overall, the hardest thing I had to do was find a new bike. I'm 6'4" and no one in Europe had a bike in stock in my size. So I had to order a bike from the U.S., with the chance it could get lost in customs. Of course, it did, but finally arrived the day before I departed for the race.

My next obstacle was learning how to swim one-handed. I practiced in the local public swimming pool and ended up swimming in circles, annoying all the old ladies, plugging along finally making it work well enough to compete. At that point, running was the last thing I had time to worry about and could only fit in the time and energy to run five or six miles before it was time to race.

On my drive down to Sherborne, where the race was being held, I wasn't worried. In the weeks since the accident I had been kidding myself into thinking that it was okay to fail because of my injury. I didn't mind going to the starting line, at least it showed that I was giving it my all. If I failed, it was because my limbs were broken. Nobody could ask me for anything more. I was feeling pretty sorry for myself with my broken arm, when the gentleman ahead of me at the registration table looked back and smiled at me. I immediately noticed that he only had one arm! At that moment

I knew I was kidding myself. It was like someone was sending me a signal. I had a broken arm, but I still had an arm. Suddenly, it wasn't an excuse anymore, and things got serious.

Once I cut my cast off and wiggled myself painfully into the wetsuit I was ready to go. The 3.8 km swim was comical, as I struggled to pass opponents with my one arm pushing them out of the way. And the bike went well, until my wound split open right at the beginning. I found that in the end, completing the Ironman was the best thing I had ever done.

You two were such an inspiration through the whole race. When I was feeling the pain or things were getting difficult, I just thought to myself, "Well the swimming wasn't that bad, because all I had to do was swim one-handed, Dick has to swim pulling Rick behind him. And the cycling wasn't that bad, because I had the best bike money could buy and Dick does it on an absolute heap of junk with Rick sitting on the front weighing him down 100 more pounds." I pushed myself, because if you guys could do it, then why couldn't I?

Dick, at sixty years old, two months postoperative after a heart attack, pulling your son along with you, you still beat my time by an hour and a half. When I share with others your DVD and book, it leaves everybody with an awe-inspiring feeling, but you can tell a difference in those who have run an Ironman because by the end they are speechless. They know how near to impossible it really is. I am glad that I can now truly appreciate how hard you two work. Since my 2005 Ironman, I have completed three more, cutting my time by an hour and fifty minutes.

With my competitive spirit and heart for entrepreneurship, I can't deny that I have started up a few more businesses in the last couple of years. The difference now is that my family comes first.

My businesses have to fit around me being a dad and not the other way around. With my new life, I am able to stay close to home and enjoy dinner with my family every night. Thank you, Dick and Rick, for allowing me to realize the importance of them.

It's bizarre that we are constantly looking for people to look up to and call heroes. We usually look toward world-class sports teams and celebrities, but then you find two normal guys in Boston and you say, "That's who I want to be like."

Dick and Rick, I want to be like you.

MIKE CHARLTON
UNITED KINGDOM

Chapter 17

Our Speaking Career

O ur personal motto, the one Rick and I have long ascribed to, is "Yes You Can." You can do anything you set your mind to. I think people naturally picked up on that refrain when they saw us racing, sweating to every finish line. Before we had done more than a few races, I started to get calls from various folks asking me to speak about our story. The requests started coming in right around 1981, just after our first Boston Marathon. By then, there had been quite a few articles and publicity about Team Hoyt on the local television stations and in the newspapers. Everyone wanted to know what Team Hoyt was all about—how we got started, why we were doing what we were doing, the usual kind of curiosity that surrounds us. Strangers would call me at home to ask me to come speak at their local get-togethers like the Rotary Club, the Lions Club, local running clubs, that sort of thing. We would get phone calls from area schools where administrators knew about Rick and his struggle to not only become an athlete but also get an education. In some ways, it was ironic that they were so anxious to listen to him, given the difficulties we had faced getting school officials to even let him into school. But it had clearly all worked out in the end, so we were glad to share our story.

We weren't paid a speaker's fee for those early engagements. It didn't occur to me that people might pay to hear me talk. I was not a motivational speaker by trade. Folks just wanted me to come and tell the Team Hoyt story, which I was very happy to do. I could spread the word about Rick's disability and how he felt more alive when he and I were running in races. Rick even wrote his own speech early on when he was in the fifth grade and still experimenting with his new TIC. He wrote a wonderful fifteen-minute speech that probably took him fifteen hours to type. *People* magazine ran a copy of it, which drew a lot of attention.

It was very difficult when I first started speaking in front of a large crowd, or any crowd for that matter. When I was in school, I was extremely shy and did not like getting up in front of the class or answering questions from the teacher. I was smart and knew the answers, but I did not like to raise my hand or volunteer information. When I was called on to answer or had to stand up in front of the class for talks, I quickly turned red and became embarrassed. I was never the cut-up Rick has always been. Instead I was bashful and preferred to remain in the background and answer my questions on my homework and on tests. As an adult, I get butterflies about every time I'm at the starting line to a race, but it's not the same anxiousness I felt when I would ascend a podium on a stage to deliver a speech. I had climbed mountains, but speaking in public was one mountain that freaked me out.

Standing in front of a crowd and knowing the audience is expecting me to say something brilliant was scary. My palms would sweat. My heart would pound, and I thought, why am I so nervous? Our story is a simple story of persistence. Ultimately, that's what I did to overcome my stage fright; I persisted. If Rick could do all that he does, then I could get up and say a few words in front of strangers. After speaking a few times, I came to realize what an incredible opportunity this was and how welcoming my audience always seemed. People embraced us and our message. People really listened and felt they could learn from our story. Society had come a long, long way. I remembered the days when Rick was a little baby and we didn't know what was wrong with him; Judy had worried about taking him outside, fearing what the neighbors might think or say. Years later, I would proudly push my son to sit on stage alongside me while I delivered a speech, and people applauded boisterously. Knowing the message was worth any discomfort I felt about public speaking, along with the outpouring of love and support, greatly lessened my stage fright.

In the beginning, Rick was not able to attend speaking events with me, as he had school and homework that kept him busy. But after a while, he was able to fit some of the talks into his schedule and enjoyed joining me on stage. He's a real ham, and he's got a compelling message of his own to deliver. When his computer was upgraded to include a voice synthesizer—Rick's first communication system with voice output was the LightWriter in 1986—he could write a speech and store it in his computer to play at these events. People could hear his thoughts—in his own words—about how he felt when he was running in events. That's always the most powerful part of any presentation we do—hearing Rick speak for himself.

Unfortunately, flying to speaking engagements is getting harder for Rick as he gets older and his back problems worsen. It is difficult for him to sit for long periods, making travel very strenuous, because his body is continually moving and shifting. Every year, those movements seem to increase a little bit more and last longer. Rick is very uncomfortable when traveling, and if his discomfort cannot be controlled with pool therapy, back massages, back braces, and muscle relaxers, he might have to have surgery within the next few years as a last resort.

Then, there's the issue of his wheelchair. (In addition to our running chair, Rick has a regular wheelchair and a traveling chair.) The airlines really demolish the traveling chair. Once, it came off the plane and was missing an arm, after being tossed in with the rest of the baggage. For the longest time, we were unable to get it fixed and specially fitted, so his traveling chair had some screws missing, an arm gone, and the parts duct-taped together. We don't want to put a brand-new traveling chair on the plane and have it get torn apart like his old one, so we often travel with the beat-up, original version. Because it has been pieced back together so many times, that chair is also very uncomfortable for Rick to sit in, and it is not fitted as well as it should be to his body. He needs to be sitting a certain way in his chair in order to control his head switch for activating his TIC and if he is not sitting correctly, he cannot control the switch correctly. So at a speaking engagement, if the way he is sitting prevents him from easily controlling the switch, the presentation is less effective. All of this forces Rick to stay home more often than he would like, at least for speaking events that require flying. He travels with me when the engagement is within driving distance as he can sit in his regular chair to be driven there in his van, but for events that require flying, I go on my own.

Our first paid speeches were in local public schools. They would have a disability awareness week—a huge victory in and of itself—and had funding to pay speakers to talk to the students in an assembly. Rick and I would go to the school, do a short presentation, and the school would give us a check for $40 or $50 to compensate for our time and travel. We never publicized our presentations, but word of mouth and all the different segments that were shown on TV helped spread our story. Before I knew it, local school officials and presidents of companies were asking me to speak to their employees. Initially, I didn't quite understand it. It made sense that we were asked to speak to the YMCA or The Arc—an organization that advocates for the rights of people with intellectual and developmental disabilities—but huge corporations that had nothing to do with people with disabilities? That's when I knew it was about the message we were spreading, not necessarily about people relating to Rick's disability. "Yes You Can" resounds with everyone, even the able-bodied. I have spoken to all kinds of companies and organizations, from Procter & Gamble to the Special Olympics, hospice programs to colleges, Goodwill Industries to Google, Inc. The message never changes, and yet the audience is receptive wherever we go.

We get many letters from people who have attended our events or from the corporations who sponsored us to come. We keep them all. The authors' willingness to thank us truly motivates us to keep doing what we're doing. For example, after speaking at the Middleboro YMCA Annual Strong Kids Breakfast, the

CEO of the Old Colony YMCA wrote to tell me that he had followed Team Hoyt over the years. He had seen us compete at the Old Colony Y's annual triathlon, but that "it was not until your presentation that I fully understood what your life's mission has called you to do." The CEO went on to say, "Remarkable would be a mild statement for what you have done by example with your son. What those efforts have meant on behalf of the disabled can only be measured by the achievements of world leaders."

Kathy Boyer, my girlfriend and also the office manager for our business, received a particularly moving e-mail from a student at Holy Cross College where I had given a talk:

> One of the young men who asked a question at the end of the talk was an autistic student who attends the college. The next day I saw him in our campus center repeating "Yes we can" to himself. As much as the talk affected me, I was truly dumbfounded by your effect on him. I doubt that [the student] will send you an e-mail, but I really wanted to reiterate the effect that seeing Dick speak had upon myself and on the rest of the students in attendance.

After I flew out to California for a special talk for a hospice program, the director quickly wrote in thanks:

> It has now been exactly one week since you visited Bakers-field as a special guest speaker at the Hoffmann Hospice fifteenth annual Voices of Inspiration fund-raiser. Words cannot begin to express the impact you made—and still leave—on each and every one of us because of your Team Hoyt presentation. Your dedication to Rick—providing him so many opportunities to experience such quality of life

despite his disabilities—closely mirrors our mission to the terminally ill patients and their family members in our community. It was an absolute blessing that you agreed to visit us on the West Coast to share your story.

How could we not be moved by such generosity, by people reaching out to let us know that we were making a difference? It's what speaking at these events was all about. Over the years, the speaking engagements kept getting bigger and bigger. Through them, I not only felt the personal satisfaction that I was using my story to motivate others, but we were able to help raise money for causes we believed in, including disability awareness.

Because the YMCA has special programs for disabled children, we have always been especially drawn to them. Once, I was asked to speak at a YMCA camp at a big breakfast event. We ended up raising over $15,000 for the organization. I challenged everyone in attendance to do what they could to raise more. When it was all over, the YMCA said that it was the most money they had ever raised at a single event. Compared to what huge corporations make on a daily basis—and the cost of running an organization like the YMCA, with all that they offer—it wasn't that much. But it was community driven, with folks in the area helping to raise the additional funds. They felt Rick and I had made an impact, and they really appreciated it.

We've also been big supporters of Easter Seals, joining with them in a "Team Hoyt for Easter Seals Campaign." As a child, Rick participated in Easter Seals' summer camps and their swim program. They've done so much for our family over the years, it was only fitting that we give something back to them. Our biggest Easter Seals payback came in 2006, when we dedicated our twenty-fifth running of the Boston Marathon to Easter Seals and partnered with the Massachusetts chapter of the organization in a yearlong effort to raise the money that would sustain them for the next several years. It was a huge success, and we raised over $360,000 for their programs through a golf tournament, raffles and auctions, T-shirt sales, and fund-raising dinners. Kirk Joslin, the president and CEO of Easter Seals Massachusetts, was thrilled and said the total amount exceeded anything he had ever imagined.

Another obvious choice for our support has been Children's Hospital Boston, because it too has been so influential in Rick's life. While many people know about my son's tremendous athletic accomplishments, many probably don't know about his long-time relationship with Children's Hospital, whose Augmentative Communication Program has helped him communicate for twenty-five years, since the initial development of the TIC by the Tufts engineers.

To thank them, in 2009, we dedicated our running of our twenty-seventh Boston Marathon (and one thousandth race) to the hospital and its Augmentative Communication Program. Rick recorded a promotional clip for the hospital, using his voice synthesizer to say, "If everybody who sees Dad and me make history could give a dollar to the Augmentative Communication Program, it would be a huge improvement to the quality of life for people who are nonspeaking." Rick and I used the Hoyt Foundation to donate $25,000 to kick off the campaign and encouraged others to donate what they could. The response has been tremendous and ongoing. Again, it is things like that—where everyone unites to create something great—that have kept Rick and I going, wanting to do more.

All of a sudden, by 2005 or so, we were in high demand. Our impact on others had evolved from inspiring people on the road to inspiring people over dinner. Between training for races and triathlons during the week, doing the races on the weekends, and flying around to speak at these company events, it was a busy time. Speaking out about our story has been so important to what we do. I feel that I can really make a difference and that anyone can if they really set their mind to it. I would be doing a disservice to Rick if I didn't spread our story.

These days, I am much more relaxed speaking in front of groups. It can be a small group of twenty, or a crowd of twenty-five thousand—the size of the audience doesn't bother me anymore. Once I get on stage and start telling our story, I am fine. What makes that possible is how welcoming those groups are. It's like getting up in front of family.

Most people I talk to get back to me and say that they cannot believe how down to earth and easy it is to get along with me. I guess they imagine me as this tough athlete, a giant on the TV screen who is pushing his son along in all these races. Before an event, when an organization's representatives pick me up at the airport, I think they are waiting for this six-foot tall, muscular guy to get off the plane. Then they see all five feet, six inches of me, and they always comment on how much shorter I am in person. Kathy warns people to look for a "short, older guy wearing running clothes." I like to joke that appearances can be deceiving. Rick can certainly attest to that.

Our story and our message are simple. Though technologies have improved, and I can accompany my talk with a PowerPoint presentation and DVDs, my general speech has stayed much the same over the years. During a presentation, I'll start off telling the audience that I want them to remember three small words: "Yes You Can." Then I get into Team Hoyt's background and how for decades, people had been telling Rick and me, "No you can't." The images we project or the short DVDs we show to break up the speech all feature Rick telling his story, with clips of him speaking through his computer. Even when Rick is unable to be there physically, the audience members can feel his presence on the stage. When he breaks into that grin of his and you can hear his laugh, it's especially powerful. It still gets to me, every time.

My ultimate goal at these events is to share my lifelong commitment to changing attitudes and educating others about disabilities. We've seen an impact because of our efforts. The best part of any speaking engagement is socializing with the groups after I speak. A surprising number of them, even when I'm talking to a group of CEOs from some big corporation, have done a race or triathlon. Others have a family member or close friend in a wheel-chair or know someone with a disability. Company executives have come up to me after a speech to say that because of our story, they are committed to trying races and triathlons—that I have motivated them to do the same in their lives. A common thread unites every audience member I speak with—all want to talk about their own stories and tell me how our story can help them to overcome some obstacle in their lives.

A young lady once came up to me and told me that there was a woman working in her office who had to use a wheelchair. This lady did not work directly with the woman, but saw her in passing enough to say hello and smile when she went by. She could have had more of a conversation with her, but felt that they would not have anything in common, as she was able to walk and move around and this other young lady was in a wheelchair. Then, the young lady said, someone e-mailed her one of the YouTube videos of us racing and the *Sports Illustrated* article written about Rick and me. She quickly realized that although Rick was in a wheelchair, he had a strong mind and a zest for life and was someone that she wanted to meet. She then came to understand that her coworker was a person, too—someone she had overlooked only because she used a wheelchair. The young woman started talking to her on breaks and at lunch and realized they had a lot in common. They liked the same kind of music and movies and enjoyed the same type of food. They started going out after work and are now very good friends. The young lady went on to say that if she had not heard about Rick's story, she never would have attempted to make friends with the woman in her office, and they both would have lost out on a great friendship.

All these amazing stories have made an impact on me. Many people cry, which chokes me up as well. It is very touching for me when they tell me how much Rick and I have affected their lives. People say they saw the speaking event on our Web site, calendar, or in a local newspaper, and have driven many hours with their families just to hear the story. They tell me how their lives have changed after hearing about us. They have become better parents; lost weight; given up alcohol, drugs, or smoking; or cut back on their work to spend more time with their families. It is incredible to think that just hearing about Rick and me would have such an impact on all these people and their lives. To this day, I am amazed. I am always drained emotionally by the end of the evening.

Our calendar of speaking engagements became so full that it started to interfere with our racing schedule. Recently, I have had to cut back, but I still love to deliver speeches as often as possible. We receive many e-mails and phone calls from all over the world from companies and groups that want us to speak to them. Right now, our busy race schedule does not have any room in it for me to travel far away, so we are concentrating on speaking in the United States. We love to get Rick to as many nearby events as possible. He is the most important part of the story that I share. Maybe when we cut back on our racing career, we will have more time for traveling and speaking engagements. But for now, Rick and I are still enjoying our weekends of races and triathlons.

DEAR TEAM HOYT:

Prior to seeing your YouTube video, I was not able to move around without a cane or wheelchair. I was afraid to leave my house because of the challenges I might face; my life was numb and paralyzed like my body. Your video inspired me to turn my life around. From you, I learned that in the sport of running and developing a team you must face all of your weaknesses and limitations. You have to learn how to embrace your obstacles so you can live stronger through them.

As an adult, I was diagnosed with multiple sclerosis, and after I saw your video, I too began running. Whoever sees the clips of you and Rick running together thinks they can do anything. When I first started out, I would run in one mile, then 3K and 5K races. By the end of my races, I would be in so much pain and so exhausted that I would collapse, but with a smile on my face because of the satisfaction I received from reaching my goal.

After I realized how powerful the YouTube video was for me, I then spread it around to everyone in the hospital where

I worked. Melissa Landry, one of our volunteers who has cerebral palsy like Rick, sold muffins around the hospital to raise money for the Children's Miracle Network. After seeing the "CAN" video, Melissa came to me and told me she didn't want me to collapse at any more finish lines. She wanted her and her wheelchair to be there to support me. She had new heroes in her life and wanted to be like Team Hoyt. At that moment, Team Lean was born.

Melissa and I both volunteer in the geriatrics department of the hospital, and we felt that the Team Lean and Team Hoyt spirit should be spread to these patients. After showing them your video, we saw changes in the way that they all looked at their own problems. Instead of complaining all the time and feeling down on themselves, they started embracing their trials and moving on. We are now training our own team, which is learning how to enjoy life in despite of the challenges they face.

After we talked more about racing, Melissa decided she not only wanted to be there for me at the end of the race, but also wanted to run the race with me and wanted me to lean on her the whole time! I completed a race the following week with Melissa and her electric wheelchair to lean on. Knowing that the wheelchair was her whole life, I was worried about using it for the whole distance of the race for fear that we would overwork it, but Melissa was so motivated that we couldn't suggest that she not participate.

Our community became enthralled with the idea of us racing. We had the support of the hospital where we worked, our running club, and our patients. After a citywide garage sale, we finally raised enough money to buy Melissa a racing chair.

At the last race, when I fell, before Melissa joined me, a woman named Phyllis Aswell came and helped me up off the concrete. She was a training coach for a running team that was working to complete a marathon. I knew instantly that I had to sign up with her, and if I made that kind of commitment to a whole group of people, I wouldn't back down. When I signed up to be part of the team, she couldn't believe my dedication to running. But I kept reminding her, I don't do this for me, I run because I want everybody to know they can do it too.

Once Melissa and I came together as Team Lean, she also began attending our practices. Everybody loved Melissa and accommodated us in every way that they could. They really believed in the message we were trying to send and were ready to do anything they could to support us in spreading that message.

An important attitude we learned from Team Hoyt is that winning first place is not the purpose of racing. Dick, you race for Rick because he loves it and it makes him feel like he's not paralyzed. I race because I love the satisfaction I receive from accomplishing a goal after accepting my weaknesses. Melissa does it because she wants to be someone's support system, much like you, Dick. We race not for medals or times, but to prove something to ourselves. Crossing that finish line. That's the medal that we want to win.

Since the beginning, Melissa and I have run six races together, one being a half-marathon, and we are still training for our full marathon early next year. I owe my health and well-being to the inspiration of your video and Melissa's support. My health has very much improved with our training five times a week and our positive outlook on life.

We are more than our disabilities. When we can embrace them and motivate others to do the same, we find a purpose for our lives rather than just dwelling on our weaknesses. You two have been such an inspiration to us, and we hope one day that we will run a race with Team Hoyt.

We will continue to spread your message,
KAREN WHITE
LAKE CHARLES, LOUISIANA

Chapter 18

Fans Worldwide

By the time the twenty-first century rolled around, Rick and I had gone global via forms of new media I had never imagined or even really understood. The new century also ushered in a few new setbacks. In 2003, I was approaching sixty-three years old and felt I was in the best shape of my life—running a road race or competing in a triathlon nearly every weekend of the year. But just a few months before the Boston Marathon, when we were down at Cape Cod, competing in a half-marathon event in Hyannis, I felt what I can only describe as a tickle in my throat and chest. It was unusual, a break from my normal physical response to training. When that tickle persisted a month (and five more races), I went to my primary care physician, Dr. Stephanie Keaney, for an EKG. When the results came back, she recommended I see a cardiologist. Dr. Joel Gore discovered that I had had a mild heart attack. The arteries leading to my heart were 95 percent blocked. If I hadn't been in such good shape, I would have been dead fifteen years earlier. Rick had truly saved my life. I had to undergo an emergency angioplasty and have stents put in, so we were forced to miss the Boston Marathon that year.

We didn't let it get us down for long. By September 2003, Rick and I were gearing up for another Ironman World Championship in Kona, Hawaii. My doctors could hardly believe it, but they all gave me a clean bill of health and the go-ahead to continue on as we'd been doing. My ticker is in great shape now and will no doubt outlast the rest of my body. Rick and I weren't going to let a little heart surgery stop us. We're used to adversity.

Unfortunately, though, it was to be the year of hospital visits. Everything was going great at Kona, but at the eighty-five mile mark on the bike leg of the Ironman, I crashed—hard. The racing bike was damaged, and Rick, banged up pretty badly in the fall, had to spend five hours in the emergency room. He came out with stitches above his right eye. Rick being hurt in a race is my worst nightmare.

A few years later, in 2005, we went through a similar rough patch. During a bad storm, a tree came through the roof and into my living room. Just days later, our specially equipped van broke down and we had to get a new one. To top off the year, I spent Christmas on crutches after knee surgery to repair cartilage damage. After all those years of running, it was the first time I had needed a repair. The media was there to record it all, the good and the bad. In many ways, it was a comfort to know that people were checking in.

I never expected so many different media outlets to be interested in telling our story. Before, the traditional media—from newspapers to newscasts—had embraced us. We had been on *TLC Amazing Families*, *60 Minutes Australia*, and *Good Morning America*. We did the *Rosie O'Donnell Show* and *Weekend Today*. Our story was out there, in the United States and abroad, and people were regularly writing or calling us to tell us their stories or to hear more about ours. Rick and I were even part of a documentary film produced by Disney, Louis Schwartzberg's *America's Heart and Soul*, which profiles a dozen different Americans deemed extraordinary.

My son and I remained somewhat oblivious to the magnitude of the attention—if only because we kept so busy. Rick was always working or preparing for upcoming events on top of his demanding daily routine. If I wasn't training for a race, I was preparing for a speech. The attention was nice, and certainly flattering, but we never set out to get on TV or have articles written about us. Much of it was accidental or simply fell into place naturally. The Boston Marathon, for instance, is always televised, so we would get coverage every year we participated. The same applied to the Ironman race. Reporters often featured our participation in the bigger races, and the Ironman organization had been our strong supporter since the first time we competed in Hawaii and even before, in Canada. In 2004, the Ironman produced the first DVD of footage from our races, which is great for Rick and me to have as a chronicle of our time racing together and something we can share with others.

In the beginning, Rick and I had had to fight just to get a place among runners. Now, athletes were happy to make a space for us, and fans lined the event route with the sole purpose of seeing us. It occurred to me one day that it wouldn't matter if we never won a race—we're just happy to finish the race. These days, our finishing times have slowed, but performing well has always been the icing on the cake—a personal victory. It was the competing and the trying that made others notice. There are superstars in the racing world, but it's not like basketball or football. Runners aren't very often household names. At a race, people see the winners go by and don't even know who they are, but they see Rick and me and there's an immediate recognition. We hear "Team Hoyt! Can we shake your hand? Can we take your picture?" I suppose that we aren't hard to pick out from a crowd. It is nice to be recognized, but more importantly, it's nice to hear what the people have to say.

After a race, I sometimes see people hanging around nearby, looking as if they want to talk to us but are afraid to come over. I motion them over, shake their hands, and introduce them to Rick. If they competed in the race, I ask how they did. Then we start talking, and that's where the real magic happens. It's in what others have to say about their lives and aspirations. The friends I have met and the stories I have heard—there aren't words to express the kind of gratitude I feel to be able to share stories with other people. And it would not have been possible without the media's help, without a few people hearing about us and thinking, 'that's a story worth telling.'

When sports columnist Rick Reilly dedicated his *Sports Illustrated* column, "Life of Reilly," to us on Father's Day 2005, things really reached a fever pitch. Reilly had never contacted us before he wrote his now famous article, "Strongest Dad in the

World." We heard from someone at *SI* about a week before the piece came out, who just wanted to give us a heads up and asked for some pictures of Rick and me to post on the Web site when the article was published. We had no idea it would become such a big deal.

I'm still not completely sure how the article came about, but we suspect it had something to do with Bill Lowe. Lowe is a board member of Special Kids, Inc., in Murfreesboro, Tennessee. It's an outpatient facility that provides care for special needs and medically fragile children whose families might not otherwise be able to afford it. Rick and I do a lot of local nonprofits and school events gratis, but because of the strains of travel, when flying is involved, we charge a presentation fee. In early 2005, however, we received a few e-mails and calls from Lowe, and something about him and the work he was doing struck a chord. Rick and I decided to fly down to Murfreesboro, waiving the presentation fee. Bill, his wife, and family put us up in a beautiful place and paid our travel expenses. We had a wonderful time visiting with them and speaking to their group. They were doing great things for area children who could really use help. Months later, Lowe mentioned that someone from the group had gotten in touch with Reilly at *Sports Illustrated* and told him he should do a piece on Team Hoyt for Father's Day. We guess that's how it all got started. The rest, of course, is history.

The response to Reilly's column was incredible. It set off a firestorm of media activity surrounding our story. The article brought a lot of recognition to Team Hoyt, and we were exposed to so many people who had never heard of us. Millions subscribe to *Sports Illustrated*. You can find it in any barber shop, dentist's office, or doctor's waiting room in America. People opened to the back of the magazine, and the column was right there. To this day, people from many different walks of life still bring up that article when they e-mail or meet us at events.

We still haven't met in person the man who made it all happen. Though we've e-mailed back and forth, I have never shaken hands with Reilly, something I really hope to do some day. The article is included in his book *Hate Mail from Cheerleaders.* He sent us a personalized copy of the book, in which he had inscribed, "To Dick and Rick, You guys made me famous! With thanks + best wishes—Rick Reilly." He was clearly being modest. Reilly told us that people still forward him the YouTube video of us, which is often attached to the article, and write, "Hey, Rick, have you seen this?" Reilly will reply, "Yeah, I've seen it. I wrote it!"

All of the sudden we were getting calls from huge networks and from strangers across the globe. I hardly knew what to make of it. I wanted to be a part of something that was making a difference, but this was on another level. But I knew that spreading our story was important. Otherwise, people wouldn't ask to hear it, and I wouldn't be in a position to be able to tell it to them.

Because of "Strongest Dad in the World," Team Hoyt was featured on *ABC World News Tonight.* The wife of one of HBO's executives saw the program and got us on *HBO Real Sports* with Bryant Gumbel. Later, that episode won an Emmy for "Outstanding Long Feature." The *Today Show* called us for a second, more intensive feature—deeming ours "the greatest love story of all time"—and that segment quickly showed up on the Internet as well. Rick and I have been on billboards from Times Square to California, a photo of the two of us with the word *devotion* spelled out beneath. It's surreal to see our images out there, larger than life.

My son had a hand, or perhaps more importantly, a voice in all this as well. In June 2007, he surprised me by writing a beautiful piece for *Men's Health* magazine titled "What My Father Means to Me." It was the first time he had publicly acknowledged in words, to such an enormous audience, how he felt about our relationship. He wrote, "[My dad] is not just my arms and legs. He's my inspiration, the person who allows me to live my life to the fullest and inspire others to do the same." To say I was touched is an understatement.

Without us knowing it was going to happen, the piece appeared on MSN's home page for Father's Day. Thousands of e-mails poured in. At one point, Kathy had five or six thousand messages awaiting her in the Team Hoyt inbox and another five or six thousand sitting in the outbox. That's when her computer crashed.

I was moved by the outpouring of support from readers who reached out to communicate. One teenager confessed that he'd been depressed and suicidal until he saw our story. A girl from the Philippines shared the story of her older sister, who also suffers from cerebral palsy. Doctors told her family that she would never walk or talk. She now does both and calls Rick her hero. Another woman wrote that we were a shining example to her generation and that she had e-mailed the YouTube link to everyone she knew. Besides the motivation I get from Rick, personal accounts like these keep me going. These people and their stories are why I can't let up.

Much of the attention, of course, was fueled by YouTube and the Internet. The original YouTube clip from the "Redeemer" Ironman DVD was quickly picked up around the world and passed from person to person, linked and forwarded via e-mail, often along with the Reilly article. People said that they had just seen it and were crying their eyes out, sending it on to all their friends, and calling their spouses and children over to the computer to watch the video with them. Businesspeople said they were in their offices with the door closed because they were crying so hard from watching our video. People say that they are firefighters, police officers, veterans of war, or criminals in jail—each moved to tears by our story. The same thing happened with the *Today Show* feature.

It's remarkable to me that I should become part of an Internet sensation at age seventy. Plenty of stories had been done on us in the United States, in newspapers and on television. When we went abroad for races, we often got coverage there as well. But now, because of the Internet, people in Tokyo heard our story—and in their own language. This sort of Web word of mouth encouraged other journalists and newscasters and writers to pick up our story. We've gotten calls from Japan, Korea, Brazil, and Russia—all hoping for an interview because of the video they had just seen. Before the Internet, that obviously could not have happened. That Rick and I have fans worldwide is a pretty phenomenal feeling.

My son and I can only hope that any public attention we continue to receive increases awareness about disabilities. I am not out to become famous. What Rick and I both aim to do is demonstrate what anyone is capable of doing if he sets his mind to it. If Rick could do it and keep me doing it right alongside him for thirty years, then anything is possible.

When we crossed the finish line of our one thousandth race, our twenty-seventh Boston Marathon, my grandsons, Troy and Ryan, were at the end, waiting to congratulate me and their uncle. "Now you can go on for another thousand," they said. I have no idea how much longer Rick and I will be able to continue doing what we're doing. I know we both still love it. Our bodies are holding up, and the thrill of racing never gets old. One thing won't change. I have no desire to run alone, and Rick has said that he can't imagine racing with anyone else. We're a team. We're still feeling good, and we're going to continue until Rick says, "Dad, I've had it."

You know, I'm just a regular guy. I mow my lawn, shovel snow from the driveway, and change the oil in our vehicles. I do the grocery shopping and cook most of our dinners. I'm like any other man in America. Only I got lucky—I have a beautiful son and an activity we can do together, despite his disability. It's been an incredible journey. I'm not a hero. I'm just a father. And all I did was tie on a pair of running shoes and push my son in his wheelchair.

Rick's Letter

Dear Dad,

I wanted to take this opportunity to write a note directly to you. The word *thanks* doesn't sound right. In fact, it sounds rather shallow as a response to all the things you have done with and for me. Because of you, my life is filled with memories—some as simple as when you took me up on rooftops when you were building chimneys, and some more adventurous, like when we have gone climbing mountains. It was amazing when I was a boy and you were in the Army National Guard, and you showed me where the missiles were housed. You let Rob, Russ, and me watch missiles being launched. Then when you joined the Air National Guard, you and the Massachusetts Air National Guard running team took me to Nebraska for the Air National Guard Marathon. There are so many more memories, all created because you didn't give up on me.

I have a list of things I would do for you if I was not disabled. Tops on that list: I would do my best to race the world championship Ironman pulling, peddling, and pushing you! Then I would push you in the Boston Marathon. And I would care for you when you get too old to care for yourself. Not because I have to, but because I want to.

I value your work ethic and all that you've taught me about never giving up. Your can-do attitude predates our racing. I know the stories about when you were growing up, living with twelve people in a very small house, how you and your brothers dug a cellar by hand to give the family more space. You have never been afraid of hard work. And you loved to compete. As you went through school, you were the captain of both football and baseball teams. What you learned on those fields has helped us so much as a team.

I think it is fantastic that other father and son teams have come along now, and I hope that those sons get as much out of their experience as I get out of my time with you. It is great that these events are allowing fathers and sons to get involved with each others' lives. And it is great that you've set such an example.

Having been raised by an amazing man like you, I have a lot of advice for fathers. Take part in your child's day-to-day care— and this is important whether your child has special needs or not. Go to doctor's appointments and therapy appointments. Take the time to get to know your child. Really know him. And don't be afraid to get dirty, even if it means getting on the floor to play with him. Try to communicate with your children. Do things together in order to discover their likes and dislikes. Do not push them into something that you like. We run together because I asked you to do it. This wasn't your passion, it is ours.

I also have some advice to the children. Keep trying to communicate with your parents. Please cooperate with your parents, doctors, and therapists. Listen to them, but don't let anyone tell you what your limits are. Never give up!

Most importantly, I hope that everyone who hears our story knows that you taught me the key to my daily life is that I believe the phrase, Yes you can!

Thanks may be shallow. But I have to thank you for being so devoted to me. I am just as devoted to you.

I love you,

Rick